OSPREY AIRCRAFT OF THE ACES® • 55

P-40 Warhawk Aces
of the Pacific

SERIES EDITOR: TONY HOLMES

OSPREY AIRCRAFT OF THE ACES® • 55

P-40 Warhawk Aces of the Pacific

Carl Molesworth

OSPREY
PUBLISHING

Front Cover
Some of the fiercest aerial fighting of the Pacific War occurred during the Allies' advance on New Georgia, in the Solomon Islands chain, as Japanese aerial forces on Bougainville attempted to neutralise the vital airfield at Munda. In one of those clashes, 1Lt Joseph J Lesicka of the 44th FS/18th FG had the rare distinction of scoring five confirmed victories in one mission to become an 'ace in a day'.

On 15 July 1943 a force of 27 Japanese bombers, with 30 to 40 Zero escorts, was reported approaching Munda from the west. Forty-four Allied fighters responded to the alert, including seven P-40s from the 44th FS/18th FG that were patrolling nearby Rendova Island when the call came.

As they reached 15,000 ft over Kolombangara, the P-40s encountered A6M Zero fighters which had scattered following an earlier clash with US Marine Corps F4Us. Flight leader Capt Frank Gaunt led his P-40s in a diving attack and took a shot at a Zero, but apparently missed. The Japanese fighter turned in front of Gaunt's element leader, Lesicka, who promptly shot it down from behind. Within the next few seconds all seven of the P-40s became involved in a running dogfight that ranged eastward toward Vella LaVella and then back to Rendova. The American pilots claimed 12.5 victories for the loss of a single P-40.

This is Lesicka's terse personal account of the battle;

'Got one Zero with a shot from the rear. Saw a torpedo bomber and over ran him on my first pass, but smoked him and on my next pass blew him up. Went after a "Betty" bomber and on my first pass his right engine started burning. An F4U made a pass and he went down on my second pass, giving me the "Betty". Then took two Zeros off a P-40's tail. I got both of them, and one was shot with one gun.'

Lesicka claimed 4.5 victories for the mission but was given credit for five. With or without the additional half share, Lesicka had become an ace, since he had scored three confirmed victories during the preceding month. His final tally for the war was nine destroyed (*cover artwork by Iain Wyllie*)

First published in Great Britain in 2003 by Osprey Publishing
Elms Court, Chapel Way, Botley, Oxford, OX2 9LP

ISBN 1 84176 536 8

Edited by Tony Holmes and Bruce Hales-Dutton
Page design by Mark Holt
Cover Artwork by Iain Wyllie
Aircraft Profiles by Jim Laurier
Scale Drawings by Mark Styling
Index by Alan Thatcher
Origination by Grasmere Digital Imaging, Leeds UK
Printed by Stamford Press PTE, Singapore

03 04 05 06 07   10 9 8 7 6 5 4 3 2 1

EDITOR'S NOTE
To make this best-selling series as authoritative as possible, the Editor would be interested in hearing from any individual who may have relevant photographs, documentation or first-hand experiences relating to the world's elite pilots, and their aircraft, of the various theatres of war. Any material used will be credited to its original source. Please write to Tony Holmes via e-mail at:
tony.holmes@osprey-jets.freeserve.co.uk

For a catalogue of all Osprey Publishing titles please contact us at:

Osprey Direct UK, PO Box 140, Wellingborough, Northants NN8 2FA, UK
E-mail: info@ospreydirect.co.uk

Osprey Direct USA, c/o MBI Publishing, 729 Prospect Ave, PO Box 1, Osceola, WI 54020, USA
E-mail: info@ospreydirectusa.com

Back Cover
This rare colour photograph shows three war-weary P-40Ks of the 18th FS/343rd FG running up on a snow-covered ramp at Amchitka, in the Aleutian Islands, in 1944. Note the extension of the Olive Drab finish onto the propeller spinner of the second machine

CONTENTS

INTRODUCTION

As the United States Army's first-line fighter aircraft in overseas service in 1941, the Curtiss P-40 bore the brunt of the early Japanese attacks in the Pacific, beginning with the devastating raid on Pearl Harbor, Hawaii. Its lack of success against the Japanese in the opening weeks of the war saddled the P-40 with a reputation as an underachieving dog of an aircraft, and to many Americans it became a symbol of their nation's lack of preparedness for war.

It is true that the Army's P-40 squadrons were rendered ineffective by the surprise attack on Pearl Harbor, and were completely wiped out in the Philippines and Java. This came at a time when the Allied nations were grasping for any tiny shred of good news from the war fronts, and this made the P-40's failures in the Pacific all the more difficult to bear. As with most dramatic events, however, there was another side to the P-40's story. It is important to recognise that it was a weapon, and that weapons are only able to damage the enemy when they are wielded with effective strategies, tactics and skill.

The US Army would have had no greater success at Wheeler Field on 7 December 1941, or at Clark Field the following day, had its squadrons been equipped with any other fighter ever built. The fact is that a warplane cannot fight when it is sitting on the ground, as most P-40s were when the Japanese attacked Hawaii and the Philippines. The American P-40 pilots who did manage to get airborne and engage the Japanese in the opening days of the war were reasonably successful, considering their complete lack of combat experience. But these pilots were few in number, and the Army brass did not fully appreciate what they had accomplished, much less capitalise on the public relations value. So the P-40's reputation suffered while the American armed forces struggled to figure out how to fight the modern air war that had been thrust upon them. Fortunately the P-40 pilots of 1942-43 turned out to be quick learners.

This book may not completely rehabilitate the P-40's reputation, because the aircraft was lacking in two key elements of fighter performance – rate of climb and service ceiling. But it will show, through the stories of the pilots who flew the P-40 in the Pacific theatre, how the Warhawk gained in effectiveness as tactics were developed to take advantage of its positive qualities. These included a robust airframe, heavy armament, a good turn of speed in level flight and the ability to out-dive any aircraft in Japanese service. Though never the best fighter in the sky, the P-40 proved itself capable of doing the job at hand.

In the Pacific, as in China and North Africa, P-40s held the line until more modern American fighters could be introduced. Warhawks remained in the fight as the tide turned against the Japanese in the Pacific, flying missions well into 1945. By war's end, USAAF P-40 pilots in the Pacific theatre had been credited with 610.5 confirmed victories over Japanese aircraft. Thirty-one of them gained confirmation for five or more kills, attaining the coveted, but unofficial, status of 'ace', and 22 more aces scored at least one of their victories in P-40s. To the aces went most of the glory, but every pilot who strapped himself into a P-40 and flew a combat mission was a hero to this writer.

If some of the stories and photographs in this book strike the reader as familiar, it is because of all the excellent work done on this subject by authors who have preceded me. I offer sincere thanks to the many veterans of service in the Pacific theatre of operations and their families who provided me with the photographs, documents and personal recollections that made this book possible. I also would like to recognise the work of researchers and authors David Aiken, William S Bartsch, Dana Bell, Steve Birdsall, J Ward Boyce, Craig Busby, John H Cloe, Stan Cohen, Jack Cook, Steve Ferguson, Frederick A Johnsen, John W Lambert, Bob MacArthur, Ernest R McDowell, John Stanaway, William H Starke and Dwayne Tabatt. Finally, the Air Force Historical Research Agency at Maxwell Air Force Base provided invaluable historical records.

Carl Molesworth
Washington
February 2003

OPENING SHOTS

The view from the cockpit of Lt Akira Sakamoto's Aichi D3A1 dive-bomber was astounding. As the Japanese pilot approached Wheeler Field, Hawaii, at 10,000 ft, he could hardly believe what he saw. Below him, parked wingtip-to-wingtip on the tarmac, sat dozens of P-36 and P-40 aircraft – the bulk of the United States Army's fighter defences for the Hawaiian Islands.

It was 0755 hrs on 7 December 1941. There were no US interceptors in the sky, nor even any telltale puffs of black smoke from anti-aircraft fire. The Imperial Japanese Navy's attack on the American naval stronghold at Pearl Harbor had achieved complete surprise. Within moments, Sakamoto's 20 raiders would begin dropping their bombs with pinpoint precision on the American fighters at Wheeler Field. Some ten miles away, other elements of the 183-aircraft Japanese strike force would begin attacking the Navy's Pacific Fleet at Pearl Harbor and the Army's bomber force at nearby Hickam Field. Like it or not – and ready or not – the United States was about to become an active participant in World War 2.

Although the timing and location of the strike came as a surprise to most Americans, the fact that an attack was imminent should have been obvious to everyone as 1941 drew to a close. In fact, Japan had been following an escalating pattern of aggression in the Pacific for ten years, starting with the invasion of Manchuria in 1931. In November 1936 Japan signed the Anti-Comintern Pact with Germany and Italy, and the following summer commenced large-scale military operations against China proper. This undeclared war had two unintended results that would weigh heavily in future events. For one thing, the war did not go as well as Japan expected, eventually turning into a stalemate that began to bleed the island nation of scarce natural resources. On the positive side for Japan, its forces were gaining valuable combat experience in China, coupled with the opportunity to test newly-developed combat equipment under operational conditions. Chief among these new weapons were the Navy's Mitsubishi A6M Zero fighter and Aichi D3A1 dive-bomber, later to receive the Allied code name 'Val'.

The outbreak of war in Europe in 1939, quickly followed by Germany's conquest of much of western Europe, created opportunities for Japan in Asia, where two of the defeated countries, France and Holland, maintained colonies in areas rich with natural resources. French Indo-China's rice, coal, tin and zinc, along with the Dutch East Indies' rubber, oil and tin, could provide Japan with the materials needed to enable it to continue the war against China. Thus was born the 'Greater East Asia Co-Prosperity Sphere', the blueprint for Japan's domination of the continent.

Throughout this period the United States, which had interests of its own in Asia, had grown increasingly aggressive in its attempts to rein in Japan by economic means. In the summer of 1940, US President Franklin Roosevelt froze all Japanese assets in his country, and soon the ABCD Powers (America, Great Britain, China and the Dutch East Indies) established a blockade which cut off 75 per cent of imports to

Japan. As pressure built, and the Japanese economy began to suffer, something had to give. Diplomatic efforts increased between the United States and Japan during the autumn of 1941, but to no avail. Meanwhile, the Japanese military was hard at work planning for war. Admiral Isoroku Yamamoto engineered an air attack on the American naval bastion at Pearl Harbor in the hope of removing the US Navy from the fight at the beginning. Invasion plans were also drawn up for the conquest of the Philippine Islands (then an American possession), the British colony at Hong Kong, French Indo-China and the Dutch East Indies.

President Roosevelt and his top military leaders were not unaware of Japan's hostile intentions because US Naval intelligence had broken Japan's diplomatic radio code some months earlier. Nor were the Americans lacking in military assets to defend Pearl Harbor from aerial attack. Of 231 military aircraft stationed on the island of Oahu, 115 were Army P-36 and P-40 fighters of the 14th Pursuit Wing to provide air defence. Army B-17 and B-18 bombers were available for patrol duties, as were Navy PBY flying boats, and a new net of radar stations provided further aerial surveillance.

At this time the Curtiss P-40 was the first-line operational fighter in the US Army Air Corps' inventory, and nine pursuit squadrons in Hawaii were fully or partially equipped with the type. The P-40 had its roots in the radial-engined Curtiss model H-75 Hawk fighter.

Designed in 1934-35, the H-75 entered service with the US Army in 1938 as the P-36. It was an excellent peacetime fighter, with pleasant handling characteristics and a top speed of just over 300 mph. By 1940, however, British and German fighters engaged in the war in Europe had performance and firepower far beyond the P-36's capabilities. Recognising the need to upgrade and expand its fighter forces, the US Army issued a request for proposals from the American aircraft industry for a new fighter that would be on a par with contemporary European designs. Curtiss proposed replacing the P-36's radial engine with the new Allison V-1710 liquid-cooled powerplant. The Army liked the idea as Curtiss would be able to produce the new aircraft quickly, and so a contract for more than 500 of the fighters was issued. Curtiss called the new aircraft the Model H-81, while the US Army designated it the P-40.

The P-40 offered an increase in top speed of nearly 50 mph over the P-36, but it suffered in other ways. Its greater weight slowed the rate of climb and reduced manoeuvrability compared to the P-36. More importantly, the Allison engine produced maximum performance at just 15,000 ft – far below the operational ceiling of contemporary European and Japanese fighters. This was not so much the fault of the engine as the product of outdated Army thinking which still saw fighters as medium-altitude, short-ranged weapons.

Despite its shortcomings, the P-40 began to arrive at Army fighter bases in May 1940. Pilots appreciated the upgrades in armament and armour protection compared to the P-36, and they were most impressed by the fighter's spectacular diving speed. In Hawaii, P-40B and C models had been supplied to most squadrons of the 15th and 18th Pursuit Groups by December 1941.

Prior to the outbreak of the war, Army pilots considered Hawaii a plum assignment. Their workdays were short, their accommodation at

Wheeler Field comfortable, and there was plenty of fun to be had during off-duty hours. Even better, they were flying 'Uncle Sam's' best fighter at that time. Among those pilots was 2Lt Francis S Gabreski of the 45th PS/15th PG, who joined the unit fresh out of flight school in April 1941. In a 1990 interview, he recalled his first flight in a P-40B;

'I just about clobbered myself, because I wasn't accustomed to the torque of the inline engine. The flight leader who was going to take me out talked at length about the P-40's idiosyncrasies, but he never did really stress the difference in torque (from the P-36). I started moving down the runway, advancing my throttle and increasing my airspeed on the ground. Then I decided to give it full throttle, all the way forward to the firewall. When I did that, boy, I got that little extra boost that I wasn't ready for, and it sort of turned the aeroplane to the left because of the torque. I wasn't alert enough on my rudder – the right rudder – to compensate for the torque, so the aeroplane started going to the left. This was still on the ground.

'The first thing that came to mind was, "I better get off the ground as fast as I can regardless", which would have been a disastrous mistake if I didn't have the flying speed. But it accelerated so fast that it just went through the transitory where it was going to the left, and as it became airborne, I kicked a little bit more rudder and sat it square as could be. So I got off alright, but it was with trepidation. So I went on and did my air work. I took the aeroplane and stalled it, just at the verge of stalling, where the aeroplane would start burbling, and I'd let the nose go down. I picked up speed and started doing a few turns, and then flew some full-powered climbs.

'Everything I did was with trepidation. It was not something that you would take to and say, "Gee,

This was the state of military preparedness in Hawaii during 1940 – little more than a year before the outbreak of hostilities. The shiny P-36A assigned to Maj Ken Walker, CO of the 18th PG, heads a line of ancient P-26s at Wheeler Field, the main US Army fighter base on Oahu Island (*Bruce K Holloway*)

Life was good for US Army personnel in Hawaii during the months preceding the Pearl Harbor attack. Here, fighter pilots of the 15th PG enjoy cocktail time at the Wheeler Field officers' club. At left are 2Lt Francis S 'Gabby' Gabreski and 1Lt Emmett S 'Cyclone' Davis, both of whom would go on to establish outstanding combat records during World War 2. The others are unidentified (*Francis S Gabreski*)

this feels comfortable. I love it". I was like a new entity. After about 50 minutes I came in and made a landing. Of course, the landing was not a very good one because I wasn't that proficient. I made a little bounce, but got it under control. Thank God that you had that sod to the left and right so that you could land on any portion of the field at Wheeler – even turn to the left or right a little – and still be on the field without running into anything. So that was an experience I'll never forget. It was not scary, but it was something that made me think that each one of these new aeroplane types had a little different personality.'

Gabreski soon tamed the P-40 and went on to become the leading USAAF ace in the European theatre in 1944. Despite his later success, he considered another pilot in his 45th PS flight, 2Lt Emmett S Davis, to be the P-40's master. Davis earned such renown for his abilities with the P-40 that he picked up the nickname 'Cyclone'. In 2001 he recalled his pre-war service in Hawaii;

'When I graduated from flight school in November 1940 (Class 40G) I was sent to Hamilton Field, and specifically the 20th PG, commanded by Col Ira C Eaker. We flew both P-36s and P-40s. In February 1941 the War Department decided to send P-36s to Wheeler Field. I volunteered for the mission. The aircraft and pilots travelled to Hawaii on the aircraft carrier USS *Enterprise*.'

On 26 February 1941 Davis was one of 30 pilots who made Army history when they performed the first launches of Army fighters from a carrier, departing from the deck of the *Enterprise* and heading for Wheeler Field . He continues;

'I was first assigned to the 6th PS/18th PG, then a few weeks later I was transferred to the 45th PS/15th PG. When I was assigned to the 45th, the squadron operations officer was 1Lt Woodrow "Woody" Wilmot. He was one of the more experienced P-36 pilots, having been sent from Selfridge Field, Michigan. He was a superb pilot, and he took me under his wing and taught me all of the clever and skilful manoeuvres that he used in our practice dogfights. The manoeuvre that proved to be the most success-ful in our mock engagements was one where you did an almost vertical climbing turn, always keeping your adversary in sight, followed by a hammerhead stall at the top and dropping down on your opponent's tail.

Future Lightning ace 2Lt George T Chandler flies in formation in 45th FS/15th FG P-40K 'White 404' over Hawaii on 8 September 1942. Chandler's combat career would take him to New Guinea and Guadalcanal (*Dwayne Tabatt*)

'New pilots arrived shortly after I did, Gabreski being one of them. He and I practised dogfighting many times in 1941. He became very good, and could beat most of the other pilots, but he never became fine-tuned enough to defeat me! At night, when the pilots met in the officers' club, dogfight challenges were issued, and I tried to accommodate most of them. It was then when someone made an off-hand remark about going to fight "the Cyclone", and that nickname has remained with me throughout the rest of my life.'

Davis and Gabreski were typical of the several hundred Army fighter pilots who were honing their skills in the skies over Hawaii as war clouds grew darker in the autumn of 1941. But when the Japanese attack finally came, only a handful of them would get a chance to fight back.

TOOTHLESS DRAGONS

For all the military hardware defending Pearl Harbor, the American forces were, as one newspaper later put it, 'caught with their pants down' by the Japanese on 7 December 1941. The US Army and Navy commanders in Hawaii had received a 'war warning' from Washington, DC on 27 November. But lacking respect for Japan's military capabilities, and an appreciation of the destructive power of a modern air attack, they decided that the greatest threat to Pearl Harbor was from local sabotage.

Accordingly, they ordered fighters and bombers to be moved out of the protective dispersal areas around their airfields and bunched up on the hangar lines where they would be easier to guard. They ordered no increase in aerial reconnaissance missions and they placed the battleships moored at the Ford Island piers on 'Condition 3', which called for partial manning of anti-aircraft batteries, while roughly a third of the ships' crews were allowed shore leave. The radar stations were on minimum manning by inexperienced or completely untrained personnel. And on Saturday 6 December all non-essential Army personnel at Wheeler Field had been given the weekend off. There was a big dance at the officers' club that night.

At 0555 hrs on 7 December, Lt Cdr Mitsuo Fuchida's strike force began launching from six Japanese carriers about 200 miles due north of Honolulu. An Army radar station on the north coast of Oahu spotted the incoming formation just over an hour later, but the pursuit officer on duty mistook the plot for a flight of B-17s due to arrive from California that morning and told the station to ignore it. Much has been made over the years of the failure to sound the alarm, but in fact 40 minutes' warning would have made little difference to the 14th Pursuit Wing's ability to defend Pearl Harbor. For on that morning the bulk of the fighter force was a 'toothless dragon', the guns of many P-36s and P-40s at Wheeler Field having been removed for safe keeping in a locked area of the main hangar. The time required to reinstall and load the guns, combined with the fighters' slow climb rate, would have made the warning academic.

At 0755 hrs Fuchida gave the order to attack. Sakamoto's 'Vals' immediately rained down their bombs on the installations and flightline at Wheeler, then began strafing the field. For 20 minutes they circled in a counter-clockwise direction, shooting up anything that looked like a worthwhile target. Lt Kiyoguma Okajima, leading a flight of A6M2 Zero fighters assigned to escort the 'Vals', decided he could add nothing to the

11

The destroyer USS *Shaw* explodes in a ball of fire at its mooring in Pearl Harbor on 7 December 1941. It was one of three destroyers sunk during the Japanese attacks

carnage below and left the area to strafe another target, the naval air station at Barber's Point. Later, a flight of Zeros from the second wave strafed the field again, but thick black smoke rising from the burning American aircraft shielded two squadrons' worth of fighters hidden from view at the west end of the flightline. Most of them survived.

When the first attack began, 'Cyclone' Davis was sleeping off a late-night poker game in the officers' quarters at Wheeler. Awakened by shouts of alarm, he quickly dressed and then hitched a ride with another pilot to the hangar area. Davis recalled;

'I ran to the flightline and proceeded to start and taxi three P-36s nearest the other burning aircraft to a safer area to the west. The fourth aircraft I got into was a P-40. The enemy attack appeared to be over, so I decided to taxi it out to the bunker that we had used when we were on alert.

'The guns in my squadron's aeroplanes had been taken out and stored in the armament shop. So after parking the aircraft in the nearest bunker, I ran to the club, got into my car and drove to the hangar. I found an armament crew chief, and he and I proceeded to break the lock on the armament shop door. We took out six machine guns, two 0.50-cals and four 0.30-cals. We loaded them in the back of my Oldsmobile sedan and drove back to the P-40 in the bunker. We installed the machine guns in the aeroplane – the two 0.50s went in the nose, synchronised to shoot through the propeller arc, and two 0.30s were installed in each wing.

'Just before we finished, a Japanese "Val" attempted to strafe us in the bunker, but I think he was out of ammunition. He was very low, less than 50 ft. The tail gunner was facing backwards in the rear cockpit, with a devilish grin on his face. When we finished loading the ammunition, I cranked up the engine and made a take-off toward the west from that

This still from a Japanese newsreel purports to show a Nakajima B5N 'Kate' torpedo-bomber flying over Hawaii on 7 December 1941 while smoke rises from the flightline of Wheeler Field below. A total of 57 aircraft at Wheeler were destroyed and 37 disabled

bunker location. After my gear was up, and as I headed toward the mountains to the west, I fired my guns briefly. A miracle happened: All of my guns worked.

'I called fighter control at Fort Shafter and told them I was airborne in a P-40. I asked if they had any instructions for me. They told me to fly to Barber's Point, which is located on the coast west of Pearl Harbor, to investigate an enemy landing that had been reported. I flew there and found no sign of a landing, which I reported to the control centre. As I flew back, I got another good look at Pearl Harbor, with several ships burning on battleship row. There also was much smoke from the Marine base at Ewa. Three more P-40s had taken off from Wheeler Field by now, and I intercepted them just south of the field. The pilots were Lts Gabreski, Shifflet and Laurence, all from my squadron, the 45th.

'I told fighter control that I now had four P-40s. They instructed me to go to Hickam Field to escort some B-18 bombers out to look for the Japanese fleet. As we approached the north-east corner of Pearl Harbor, the Navy guns that were functional started shooting at us. I turned the flight back toward Wheeler and told fighter control that they would have to get the Navy gunners under control before any escort would be available. After we landed and refuelled, I led two more patrol flights that day. They were all uneventful.'

Although Davis and the others from the 45th PS got airborne too late to catch the withdrawing Japanese attackers, 14 Army fighter pilots did manage to engage the enemy on 7 December, flying a total of 18 sorties. In nine, P-36 pilots were credited with four confirmed victories for the cost of one shot down and its pilot killed. In addition, most of the other P-36s suffered varying degrees of battle damage. Two pilots of the 44th PS and three from the 47th PS flew a total of nine P-40 sorties during the Japanese raids.

It is significant that the 44th and 47th squadrons made all the P-40 encounters, because neither unit was based at Wheeler at that time. Thus both were spared the first wave of Japanese attacks. The 44th had 12 P-40s at Bellows Field, but only three of its pilots were on the base that morning. A single strafing pass by Zeros at about 0900 hrs killed one pilot in the cockpit of his aircraft on the ground and caught two P-40s just taking off. Both were quickly shot down, with one pilot being killed and the other wounded.

The 47th PS was more fortunate. Its mixed complement of 18 P-40s and P-36s were at Haliewa, an auxiliary field on the coast about ten miles west of Wheeler, where the squadron had been undergoing gunnery training. Japanese intelligence was unaware of the airfield, and it was not therefore targeted. Most of the unit's officers had deserted their tents at Haliewa on Saturday evening in favour of far more comfortable accommodation

The barracks building at Wheeler Field was heavily damaged during the 7 December 1941 attack, but casualties were relatively light, with 31 enlisted men losing their lives as a result of the Japanese bombing attacks

at Wheeler. When the bombs began to fall on the latter base on Sunday morning, 2Lts George S Welch and Kenneth M Taylor of the 47th PS called Haliewa to alert the men there, and to order that their P-40Bs be prepared for flight. Then they leaped into Taylor's car and sped across the island toward the base, dodging a couple of strafing attacks on the way. Several other 47th pilots followed a few minutes later.

When Welch and Taylor reached Haliewa, their fighters were ready, and they took off shortly after 0830 hrs. Their twin 0.50-cal nose guns were not loaded because there was no ammunition for them at Haliewa, so as they headed east towards the smoking ruins of Pearl Harbor, the two pilots knew they would have to make do with just the four 0.30-cal wing guns. Reaching Ewa, the pair spotted about 20 D3A1 'Vals' strafing the Marine base. Welch, the high-spirited son of an influential DuPont research scientist, gave the following account of his first encounter with enemy aircraft;

'I was leading and peeled off first. Lt Taylor was about 200 yards to the rear and side, following me. Their rear gunners were apparently shooting at the ground because they didn't see us coming. The first one I shot down, the rear gunner didn't even turn around to face me. I got up close enough to see what he was doing. I got him in a five-second burst – he burned right away. I left and got the next aeroplane in the circle, which was about 100 yards ahead of me. His rear gunner was shooting at me. One bullet put a hole through my cooling radiator and I got one in the nose. It took three bursts of five seconds each to get him. He crashed on the beach.'

Ken Taylor's account of the flight reveals his inexperience at aerial combat;

'The first aircraft I shot at burst into flames immediately, rolled over in a ball of fire and dove into the ground near Ewa Field. I then proceeded up the string, catching the next "Val", which also went down quite easily. By that time the formation was in general disarray, and I had completely lost track of George. I then tagged on to a third "Val" that was offshore near Barber's Point. I pulled up very close to this aircraft, with the rear gunner plainly visible firing at me. Because of the close proximity, I saw that he was killed with my first burst. However, despite all the hits that I was getting, this aircraft did not burst into flames as the others had, but started a gradual descent, smoking badly. Although I turned for home, this aeroplane also undoubtedly went down into the sea.

'It was most frustrating at this point to find I was out of ammunition at a time when these much slower aircraft were making a hasty retreat to their carrier. With more ammunition, or more judicious use earlier, I could have caught and destroyed several more of them.'

Welch and Taylor landed at Wheeler to rearm and refuel. At about 0930 hrs, a flight of 'Vals' approached the base intent on strafing, and

Assigned to Hawaii straight from flight school in the summer of 1941, John E Little learned the fighter pilot's trade as a member of the 46th PS, before transferring to the 44th PS as a flight leader. Here, he poses with his P-40D 40-367 *Ginia* in Hawaii prior to the squadron's deployment to Guadalcanal. Little would assume command of the 44th FS on 25 May 1943 (*John Little via Jack Cook*)

P-40 pilots 2Lt Ken M Taylor (left) and 2Lt George S Welch of the 47th PS together accounted for six Japanese aircraft shot down on 7 December 1941. Scrambling from the remote base at Haliewa in two P-40Bs, they were among the first pilots to confront the enemy, and were both awarded the Distinguished Service Cross for their exploits. Both men added to their scores later in the war, Welch finishing the conflict as a 16-victory ace. They posed for this publicity photo in front of a P-36 shortly after the attack on Pearl Harbor

Welch took off immediately with another partial load of ammunition, but unrefuelled. Taylor was a few moments behind him – just long enough for the 'Vals' to begin their strafing runs. Taylor made his take-off run directly at the oncoming Japanese bombers and began firing as soon as his wheels left the ground. Picking up speed, he made a tight chandelle and happened to roll out behind the next-to-last 'Val' in the line. Taylor started firing just as the last 'Val' started shooting at him. The P-40 pilot took some hits, including a bullet through his left arm, but Welch dropped in line behind the 'Val' and shot it off Taylor's tail. Though wounded, Taylor chased the retreating 'Vals' out to sea until he expended the last of his ammunition. Welch flew to Ewa, where he spotted a lone 'Val' and shot it down just off the beach at Barber's Point.

Welch went up a third time that morning, accompanied by 2Lt John Dains of the 47th PS in a P-36. Earlier, Dains had made two sorties in a P-40 from Haliewa and apparently shot down a Japanese bomber in a combat witnessed by personnel at the Kaawa radar station. The Japanese raiders had cleared the area by this time, but the airspace over Oahu was still a dangerous place to be. As Dains approached Wheeler Field to land, he was fired on by jumpy anti-aircraft batteries at Schofield Barracks and crashed to his death on the golf course.

Welch was credited with four confirmed victories on 7 December, Taylor got two and Dains one. Taylor and Welch still had plenty of air combat in front of them, the former serving as a flight commander in the 44th FS on Guadalcanal in 1943. Welch went to New Guinea to fly P-39s in the 8th FG, scoring three victories on 7 December 1942, exactly one year after his Pearl Harbor exploits, to become an ace. He finished the war

1Lt James O Beckwith (top row centre), CO of the 72nd FS, poses with pilots of his squadron in Hawaii in early 1942. These men are, front row from left to right, Bill Waldman, Joe Powell, Beckwith, Bob McCabe, Pappy Sawyer and Bill Feiler. Back row from left to right, Bill Haney, Roy Wigley, Bill Martin, John Cox and John Simonton. Wigley and Cox would not survive the war. The aircraft behind them is Beckwith's brand new P-40E, named *Squirt* after his daughter (*Jack Lambert*)

2Lt Robert W 'Todd' Moore flies over Hawaii in his P-40K 42-45746 *Stinger* of the 78th FS/18th FG in the summer of 1943. Moore soon transferred to the 45th FS to take part in the central Pacific campaign, during which he scored his only P-40 victory on 26 January 1944. Moore was credited with 11 more victories while flying P-51s from Iwo Jima in 1945 (*Todd Moore via Jack Lambert*)

2Lt Joseph J Lesicka, seen here posing in front of a 15th FG P-40B in 1942, was one of the many young fighter pilots who trained in Hawaii prior to joining combat units engaged in the Pacific campaign. Assigned to the 44th FS/18th FG on Guadalcanal in February 1943, Lesicka scored nine confirmed victories in P-40s (*Jack Cook*)

with 16 victories and became a test pilot for North American Aviation after the war. He was killed while testing an F-100 in October 1954.

In all, the five P-40s which became airborne during the Pearl Harbor attack shot down seven of the attackers, while losing two of their own with one pilot killed. Statistically, the P-40's combat debut in US Army service might be considered a success. But as a practical matter, the P-40 interceptor force had failed in its assigned task of defending Pearl Harbor from air attack. Perhaps undeservedly, the P-40's reputation received an indelible black mark, one that would darken in the days ahead.

The Japanese attack had shattered the battleship forces of the US Navy's Pacific Fleet. Similarly, the 14th Pursuit Wing lost 61 P-40s and P-36s destroyed, plus 41 disabled. Had the Japanese sent a third wave of attackers in the afternoon, only 38 Army fighters would have been available to intercept them. But the Japanese did not return – not on 7 December, not ever. The Army fighter squadrons at Hawaii quickly shifted to wartime status, and their aircraft losses were soon made good with later models of the P-40 and P-39. Hawaii became a major training centre, preparing fresh Army pilots for combat assignments throughout the Pacific theatre in the nearly four years of war that lay ahead.

'SUICIDE SQUADRON'

Word of the Pearl Harbor attack was flashed by radio to the headquarters of Gen Douglas MacArthur in Manila shortly after Japanese bombs stopped falling on 'Battleship Row' in Hawaii. It was 0355 hrs on 8 December local time in the Philippine Islands, and within hours a Japanese triumph even greater than the destruction of the American fleet at Pearl Harbor would begin to unfold. Again, the task of providing air

This rare P-40D was assigned to the 318th FG at Bellows Field, Hawaii, in late 1943. Its number suggests it was the personal aircraft of the group commander. Note the four wing guns, plus bomb racks (*Jim Sullivan*)

defence would fall primarily to P-40s, and once more the sturdy fighter's reputation would be tarnished by failures not of its own making.

On paper, the fighter strength deployed by the Far East Air Force's V Interceptor Command on Luzon in early December 1941 looked substantial. Of approximately 100 P-40s in four squadrons, 75 per cent were new E-models, which featured the uprated Allison V-1710-39 engine, a revised fuselage and armament of six 0.50-cal wing guns. The

20th PS flew P-40Bs identical to the ones which equipped Hawaiian squadrons, but the 34th PS had even more outdated Seversky P-35As. These squadrons were units of the 24th PG, which was based at Nichols Field, just south of Manila, along with the 17th and 21st PS. The other three squadrons were dispersed at Del Carmen, Clark and Iba airfields, all north-west of the city. In addition, a radar station was in operation at Iba, on the west coast of Luzon.

But the 24th PG was far from ready for war. Its obsolete P-35As at dusty Del Carmen had been in service for nearly two years and were worn out. The 20th PS P-40Bs at Clark Field, delivered in the summer of 1941, were in good condition, but their guns had never been fired. The P-40Es were brand new, and subject to several teething problems, including engine fires. In addition, mechanics had complied with an unexplained Wright Field technical order to disable the hydraulic gun-charging system. As a result, the guns could only be charged manually on the ground prior to take-off, so it was impossible for the pilots to re-charge their guns in flight if they jammed. In the 17th PS, only the guns of commanding officer 1Lt Boyd D 'Buzz' Wagner's P-40E had ever been fired at all – and his was the most experienced unit in the command.

The 21st PS, with the 34th, had just arrived in the Philippines two weeks earlier but had started to fly P-40Es on 4 December. The 3rd PS, at remote Iba, had further problems because the oxygen systems in its two-week-old P-40Es were inoperable, so the pilots could not fly them above about 15,000 ft. Just as important, many of the pilots were straight from flying school, and unfamiliar with their P-40s. Even the most experienced pilots in the 24th PG acknowledged that they lacked training and practice in combat tactics, and that their radio communications were feeble.

Meanwhile, 300 miles north of Manila on the island of Formosa, Japan had amassed a force of nearly 200 A6M Zero naval fighters, 200 Navy bombers and about 150 Army aircraft. Many of the men who flew them were veterans of combat in China. They were well trained, they knew their aircraft and they were eager to fight for their country.

Tensions had been building in the Far East for several weeks before the Pearl Harbor attack, with unidentified aircraft, presumably Japanese, being seen over Luzon as early as 27 November. Then, on 6 December, Col Harold George, chief of staff of V Interceptor Command, gathered

2Lt Charley Sneed is seen with 20th PS P-40B 'Yellow 53' at Clark Field, in the Philippine Islands, in 1941, prior to the Japanese attack. Other than the aircraft number on the nose in yellow, it is bereft of individual markings. Sneed commanded the Bataan Field flying detachment in January-February 1942, and was later captured on Mindanao by the Japanese (*Nora Sneed Sparks via William S Bartsch*)

his pilots at Nichols and Clark to tell them that he expected war to begin in a matter of days. Aware of the Japanese forces arrayed against them, George added this prophetic warning to his pilots – 'You are not a suicide squadron yet, but you are damned close to it.'

Still, despite ample warning of attack, US Army air units in the Philippines were all but wiped out on 8 December. Inexperience, poor communications and the competence of the Japanese attackers all played a part, but old-fashioned bad luck was a factor as well. A ground fog on Formosa delayed the Japanese strike force for several hours that morning. This allowed the P-40s and B-17s at Clark Field just enough time to take off on patrol, exhaust their fuel supplies and return to base before the Japanese raiders arrived at about 1220 hrs. At the same time, a second Japanese formation caught Iba Field equally by surprise. Within minutes, most of the P-40s of the 3rd and 20th PSs were reduced to junk, along with the bombers on Clark Field.

Meanwhile, the 17th PS, and most of the 21st PS, had been circling over Manila Bay on orders from 24th PG headquarters. A handful of P-40 pilots managed to engage enemy aircraft during the day, and each got a nasty shock when they saw the climbing and turning performance of the previously unknown A6M Zero fighters. Nine victories were credited to five pilots (plus one by a P-35A), but several P-40s were shot down and nearly all suffered battle damage at the hands of the Zero pilots.

One of the three 20th PS pilots who managed to get airborne at Clark was 2Lt Randall D Keator, who was credited with the first victory of the Philippines campaign when he destroyed a Zero which exploded after a head-on pass about 30 miles west of the airfield. He then got another a few minutes later. It was the first time he had ever fired the guns of his P-40B. A pilot who missed out on the action, but who would see plenty in the weeks to come, was 2Lt John H Posten of the 17th PS. He recorded his 8 December experience in his diary four days later;

'My flight was on alert at Nichols Field when news came through about the attack on Pearl Harbor. I guess it was at about ten o'clock that morning that we got orders to send a couple of flights to patrol north of Clark Field. There were supposed to be some bombers on their way south from Formosa. I did not go on the patrol flight. The Japs bombed Baguio, but our patrol missed them. At 1245 hrs they bombed Clark Field and Iba, and did a nasty job on both. They bombed and strafed for 45 minutes, which is a long time. Just before dark that night we received orders to move to Clark Field, because they figured Nichols would get it that night.

'When we got to Clark Field I couldn't see how we were ever going to land – everything in sight was burning and the field was covered with bomb holes. What men were left on the ground marked the holes for us, and we finally could see a place just big enough to land in. I landed with the rest, but found it was the 21st PS instead of the 17th, which is my outfit. The 17th had received orders over the radio to go to Del Carmen, about 15 miles south of Clark. My radio was not working. That night

Four pilots of the 20th PS strike nonchalant poses beside a P-40B at Clark Field in August 1941. They are, from left to right, Lts Carl Gies, Max Louk, Erwin Crellin and Varian White. Louk would die on the first day of hostilities in the Philippines, and only Gies would survive the war. Note the fighter's total lack of unit markings (*Dorothy W Tilforth via William S Bartsch*)

everything was confusion. The hangars were still burning, and every once in a while a lot of ammunition would go off that had been stored there. Automobiles, trucks and aeroplanes were wrecked and burning all over the place. All the wounded had been taken away, but the dead were still lying where they fell. That night we all went into the hills to sleep.'

As dawn broke on 9 December, only 58 P-40s remained in operational condition. But the air over the island was relatively quiet as fog on Formosa again curtailed Japanese operations. Still, at least five P-40s were destroyed in accidents caused by the poor operating conditions. Japanese troops landed at two points on northern Luzon the next day, and on 12 December another landing force came ashore at the south end of the island. By that time further dogfights and bombing raids had pared the 24th PG down to only about 25 operational fighters, despite valiant efforts by hard-working groundcrews to patch up and rebuild wrecked aircraft. Facing a growing need for aerial reconnaissance, MacArthur ordered his pursuit pilots to avoid further combat to save their P-40s for reconnaissance missions. In five days the Japanese had effectively destroyed the air defence of the Philippines.

One bright spot emerging from the gloom of the Philippines campaign was the emergence of the first Army fighter ace of World War 2 in the form of 1Lt Buzz Wagner of the 17th PS. The 25-year-old Pennsylvanian, who had brought his squadron to the Far East in November 1940, was frustrated at having missed the action on the first day of the war.

On 12 December he flew a lone reconnaissance mission to Appari, in northern Luzon, about 200 miles north of Clark Field, where the Japanese had established an air base. Two Army Ki-27 'Nate' fighters attacked Wagner's P-40E as he approached the field. Wagner climbed up directly into the morning sun, then rolled onto his attackers' tails when they lost him in the glare. The two 'Nates', flying close together, both burst into flames and went down when Wagner opened fire on them. He made two strafing passes over the field, setting five parked aircraft on fire, then was chased home by three more 'Nates'.

On 16 December Wagner scored what was hailed by Far East Air Force (FEAF) as his fifth victory. That morning, a reconnaissance mission had revealed the presence of 29 enemy fighters on the airfield at Vigan – the site of the Japanese landings on the northwest coast of Luzon. Wagner and 2Lt Russel Church took off at daybreak from Clark Field, their P-40Es loaded with six 30-lb fragmentation bombs under their wings. A third P-40E, flown by 2Lt Allison Strauss, would provide top cover.

Heavy ground fire greeted the diving P-40s, and Church was shot down after releasing his bombs on the target. Strauss then joined up with Wagner, and the two made several strafing passes over the field. On the last, a Ki-27 managed to get airborne in front of Wagner's P-40. The 17th PS commander rolled his P-40 onto its back to get a better view of the 'Nate', throttled back to keep it in front of him, then opened fire with the last of the ammunition in his six 0.50-cal guns. The Japanese fighter immediately crashed into the ground and Wagner turned for home.

On 22 December 1941 the Japanese made another landing on Luzon, this time at Lingayen Gulf, just 70 miles north-west of Clark Field. By this time the 17th and 20th PSs were down to six flyable P-40s each, and a full-force air strike was organised. Wagner led the 17th, with future ace

The US Army's first ace of World War 2, 1Lt Boyd D 'Buzz' Wagner relaxes on a beach in the Philippines prior to the outbreak of hostilities. Wagner, CO of the 17th PS, scored his fifth confirmed victory on 16 December 1941, and went on to amass a total of eight kills. He died in a flying accident in Florida on 29 November 1942 (*Alda E Childers via William S Bartsch*)

2Lt Bill Hennon as his wingman, but the formation immediately became separated in the dark and the two P-40s proceeded to the target area alone. They dropped their bombs among landing barges on the beach, then circled back for a strafing pass in the face of heavy ground fire, before being jumped by a gaggle of Ki-27s. In the ensuing dogfight, Wagner's P-40E took numerous hits, including one that shattered the windshield, spraying glass into his face and eyes, and another which hit him in the shoulder. Wagner managed to return to Clark Field, escorted by another future ace, 2Lt George E Kiser, but his injuries were severe enough to require his evacuation to Australia for treatment.

Once recovered, Wagner joined the 8th FG in New Guinea, flying P-39s. On 30 April 1942 he shot down three Zeros, bringing his final score to eight confirmed victories. He was killed in a P-40 crash after returning to the US in November 1942.

Although Wagner was the only ace of the Philippine campaign, several future ones scored their first victories during this period. These included Ed Kiser, Capt Grant Mahony of the 3rd PS and 2Lt Jack Donalson of the 21st PS. Another top scorer was 2Lt John Posten, who claimed 3.5 victories in the Philippines. The last of these came on 9 February 1942, by which time American forces had been bottled up on the Bataan Peninsula and were down to seven P-40s. Posten wrote in his diary of the five-aeroplane mission from Bataan Field;

'Took off at 0115 hrs today to protect Capt Villamor (a Philippine Air Force pilot) in an old O-1. He was to take pictures of Jap artillery positions that had been shelling Corregidor. He got the pictures okay and landed, and so did Bob Stinson, but the rest of us were jumped by six Jap pursuits. We had a helluva fight right over the field. Everyone saw it, and says it was the best show of the war. We got credit for knocking down five and maybe all six. Earl Stone is missing. My ship was shot up a little and

24th PG mechanics gather in front of two P-40Es in a revetment at Bataan Field in January 1943 to have their photograph taken by Brig Gen Harold S George, CO of V Interceptor Command. Most of these men would be taken prisoner at the end of the Philippines campaign and participate in the infamous Bataan Death March (*Jesse K White via William S Bartsch*)

I landed at San Jose because I wasn't sure our field was open. They thought I was gone, too, when I didn't show up. I waited until after dark to come back.'

None of the American pilots involved in the 9 February fight filed combat claims, but FEAF Headquarters awarded six confirmed victories to them, including one credited to Posten. The heroics of American P-40 pilots in the Philippines were not limited to missions involving air-to-air combat, however. In mid-February, Capt William E 'Ed' Dyess, CO of the 21st PS, was placed in command of the small fighter force remaining on Bataan after having spent several weeks as a provisional infantryman. He soon gained notoriety for the daring one-man bombing raids he performed in his battered P-40E, which he named *KIBOSH*. In 1943, Dyess wrote this account of the end of his battle to hold Bataan;

'The 21st PS was ordered to take over Bataan and Cabcaben Fields. At that time we had five aeroplanes, plus two old civilian aeroplanes. We used these for bombing, strafing, recon work, dropping propaganda, dropping ammunition and medical supplies to the guerrilla forces, ferrying in medical supplies in the southern islands, as fighters against Japanese aircraft, and my P-40 had a camera rigged in the baggage compartment for aerial photographs. With the exception of this P-40, we eventually lost all of these aeroplanes – however, not one was damaged by enemy bombing or strafing. Another aeroplane was put together from parts of dilapidated P-40s, and two P-35s were flown to Bataan from Mindanao. At the fall of Bataan we still had this dilapidated equipment, which I sent to Mindanao. After the aeroplanes had been sent south with as many pilots as we could possibly get in them, the squadron reverted to infantry and the equipment on the field was destroyed.'

Following his capture by Japanese troops on 10 April 1942, Dyess took part in the infamous Bataan 'Death March' and was then held as a prisoner of war for nearly a year. On 3 April 1943 he led 12 prisoners in a daring escape from Davao prison colony and linked up with guerrilla forces on Mindanao Island. He fought with the guerrillas for four months before being evacuated by submarine in July. He was killed in a P-38 crash in California on 22 December 1943.

The 37th, and last, confirmed victory by a P-40 pilot in the Philippines occurred on 12 April 1942, when Lt John Brownewell of the 17th PS shot down a Japanese floatplane near Del Monte, on Mindanao. The campaign ended on 6 May 1942, when starving American forces in the island fortress of Corregidor surrendered. After six months of defeat in the Pacific, the United States was shocked by the course taken by the war to this point, and was desperate to hear something hopeful from the war fronts. But Japan's campaign to conquer the Pacific region had reached its peak, and soon the tide would turn in favour of the Allies. P-40 pilots would then be ready to create their fair share of good news for the folks back home.

Japanese troops inspect a captured P-40E of the 24th PG on Mindanao in May 1942. Mechanics at Maramag painted the nose of the Warhawk a lighter colour and decorated it with a sharkmouth and eye during the final days of the campaign. It was one of only two P-40s which survived to be captured (*Hal Hitchcock via William S Bartsch*)

BACKS AGAINST THE WALL

On the afternoon of 31 December 1941, a twin-engined Beechcraft transport aircraft lifted off from Bataan Field, in the Philippines and headed south, bound for Australia. On board were seven fighter pilots of the 24th PG who had been chosen to lead flights of replacement P-40s to the Philippines. Five more pilots followed the next day, headed for Brisbane. But these veterans were not the only American P-40 pilots on their way to Australia in January 1942. Two complete P-40 pursuit groups, the 49th and 51st, were travelling by ship and two P-39 groups would follow in a few weeks. The 51st PG would continue to India to join the Tenth Air Force, while the 49th would join the Fifth Air Force in Australia and ultimately become the war's top-scoring USAAF fighter group.

The 49th arrived in Australia on 28 January 1942 and immediately began assembling 100 P-40s while its pilots completed their training. Meanwhile, the Philippines veterans received a new assignment after their two-week journey. The Japanese advance had moved so rapidly that the route was no longer open for ferrying short-ranged P-40s from Australia north to Bataan. Instead, the veterans were formed into the 17th Pursuit Squadron (Provisional) and told they were going to Java, where the Dutch were under increasing threat of Japanese air attacks.

Maj Charles A 'Bud' Sprague, former operations officer of V Interceptor Command in the Philippines, who had flown out in the second group, was chosen to command the new 17th PS (P). With 17 P-40Es available, Sprague picked four USAAF pool pilots and quickly made plans to head north to Java. The P-40s left Brisbane on 16 January 1942, followed by a cadre of ground personnel in C-47 transports, and arrived in Soerabaja, Java, on 25 January. Attrition on the difficult trip had reduced the number of P-40s to 13.

One of the pilots involved was 1Lt George E Kiser, a Philippines veteran with two victories to his credit, both scored during the first week of the war. He wrote this account of the Java campaign after he returned to the US in 1943;

'Our squadron in Java consisted of about 17 P-40Es with pilots. The enlisted men assigned to this

1Lt George E 'King' Kiser became the first ace of the 17th Provisional PS in Java when he shot down his fifth Japanese aircraft on 24 February 1942. With the fall of Java, he joined the 8th FS/49th FG in Darwin and flew this P-40E, which featured fuselage art showing a lion with a Zero in one paw and its pilot in the other. Kiser scored nine confirmed victories in P-40s. He flew a second combat tour later in the war, flying P-47s with the Ninth Air Force, but did not add to his score (*Young via Steve Ferguson*)

squadron consisted of one crew chief and one armourer per aeroplane, three radio mechanics and a first sergeant. We joined this crew at Darwin and escorted the C-47s, which did our navigating across to Soerabaja. The enlisted men took their tool kits, an extra aileron or two, a couple of spare tyres and nuts and bolts of assorted sizes. This, together with what we could salvage from the accidents we had, was the extent of our maintenance equipment during our six-week stay there. The enlisted men proved themselves past masters at improvising and worked constantly to keep the few P-40s we had flying. Our successes are attributed greatly to their ingenuity in maintaining the aeroplanes with practically nothing.

'Soon after we arrived in Soerabaja we moved to Blimbing, a newly constructed (and well camouflaged) field. All our future activity in the Netherlands East Indies was conducted from this field. The Japanese did not find this base until the day we were leaving for Australia. Here, we lived in the little town (Djombang) in some vacated Dutch houses about three miles from the field. The Dutch assisted us in every way possible, furnishing guards on the field, food and medicine. Living conditions were not too bad.

'We flew many missions from Blimbing Field. In fact, a lot of us flew about 150 hours during the short stay there. At all times we were outnumbered at the least 10-to-1, but still we managed to get official credit for in excess of 65 victories (the currently accepted total is 49), with only a loss of nine pilots killed or missing.

'Our activities ranged from Palembang, Sumatra, where we went to bomb and strafe the airport there, to Koepang, Timor. On 1 March 1942, the Japanese landed on Java in force, and after attacking this huge armada of ships with only ten P-40s, it was decided that the situation was hopeless, so the entire squadron retreated, along with the 19th Bombardment Group, to Sydney, Australia. We turned our aeroplanes over to the Dutch. However, it is improbable that they got any service out of them as each one was almost past the flying stage after our last raid. Only three or four P-40s were considered flyable when we finished that mission.'

This was the second P-40E named *West Palm Beach PLAY-BOY* to be flown by Lt Clyde H 'Smiley' Barnett Jr during his time with the 8th FS/49th FG. The fighter's markings included the number 55 on the fin in white and a white outline on the *US ARMY* titling under its wings. Barnett scored four confirmed victories and rose to become squadron operations executive officer (*Iling via Steve Ferguson*)

Capt Grant Mahony wouldn't stop fighting. He flew in the Philippines, scoring his first victory on 8 December 1941, then added three more while flying with the 17th Provisional PS in Java, before becoming an ace in the CBI. Shown here in 1943 while commanding the 76th FS in China, Mahony later flew with the 1st ACG in India and the 8th FG in the Philippines, where he was finally killed in action on 3 January 1945 (*Molesworth collection*)

Kiser assumed command of the 17th PS (P) a few days after Sprague was shot down and killed over Bali on 20 February 1942. During Kiser's six weeks in Java he was credited with three more victories, reaching ace status when he shot down a Japanese bomber raiding Soerabaja on 24 February. After returning to Australia he was assigned to the 8th PS/49th PG, scoring four more victories in the defence of Darwin to bring his final total to nine victories.

The top scoring 17th PS (P) pilot was 2Lt William J Hennon, who scored five victories between 3 February and 26 February. Like Kiser, he would continue to score with the 49th FG. Other future aces who scored in the Java campaign included Capt Grant Mahony and Lts Andrew J Reynolds, William L Turner, Joseph J Kruzel and James B Morehead. Mahony and Turner would go on to fly P-40s in the China-Burma-India theatre (CBI), while the others went to the 49th FG. One 17th PS (P) pilot and Philippines veteran who nearly became an ace was 1Lt Nathaniel H 'Cy' Blanton. He wrote this about the Java campaign;

'We had been at Blimbing about two days when the enemy activity started. Once started, it came fast and furious. Flying defensively, ours were not long missions – usually from one to two-and-a-half hours. On some days there would be as many as four missions, but usually two or three. Our working day started at 0400 or 0500 hrs. We were served coffee at the old sugar mill by Dutch ladies, then went to the field to aid our crew chiefs in the morning inspection of the aircraft, at which time we taxied out to take-off position and sat alert in, or near, our aircraft. Our time to leave the field varied slightly each day depending on the weather. Usually by 1700 hrs the sky was completely overcast, with very heavy thunderstorms. Because of this daily occurrence, the island was not attacked at late evening or night.

'Our total strength of aircraft when we moved to Blimbing was 12, but that was gradually built up by the addition of other flights that came to us from Australia. Our strength of pilots was always slightly more than our aircraft because we didn't lose as many pilots in combat as we did aircraft. For most of the period of our stand in the Netherlands East Indies, some of the men had boils, which were thought to have resulted from our diet. I had a total of seven, although they did not interfere with my going on every mission I was scheduled for. On a few occasions I led the squadron. Once (17-18 February) the squadron was split and Bud Sprague took half of the aircraft to the other end of the island to strike at Sumatra. On this occasion I remained behind to lead the other half of the squadron in our daily defensive missions. This day we got lucky, as we shot down nine Jap bombers without the loss of a pilot.'

Blanton's score on 18 February was one Zero fighter and one bomber destroyed. He shot down one more bomber before evacuating to Australia, where he was appointed commander of 'A' Flight in the 7th PS/49th PG. He scored his fourth, and last, victory plus a probable on 14 June 1942 and returned to the US several months later.

Despite fighting against overwhelming odds in a lost cause, the 17th PS (P) holds the distinction of being the first USAAF fighter squadron to achieve success against the air forces of Japan. Learning from the mistakes made in Hawaii and the Philippines, Bud Sprague and his squadron developed an air-raid warning system in cooperation with the Dutch and the Javanese natives, which prevented the Japanese from destroying the 17th's P-40s on the ground. They also developed hit-and-run combat tactics in the air to make the best use of their P-40s' performance characteristics, scoring 49 confirmed victories for the loss of 17 fighters. These lessons would prove invaluable in the months ahead as the survivors of the 17th played key roles in the air defence of Darwin.

STORM OVER DARWIN

On 19 February 1942, Australia suffered its own version of the Pearl Harbor attack when the Japanese Navy's land and carrier-based aircraft struck the northern port of Darwin in two devastating raids. A convoy of ships loaded with equipment and troops bound for the defence of Timor Island was caught in the harbour and mostly destroyed. Dock facilities, a nearby airfield and even a hospital were bombed, with great loss of life. Ten P-40Es of the newly-formed 33rd PS (P) were in Darwin at the time to escort the convoy while en route to reinforce the 17th PS (P) in Java, but nine of these fighters were destroyed in the air and on the ground during the day. Only one American pilot was able to make a claim.

Lt James A 'Duckbutt' Watkins flies over Darwin in his first P-40E, 'White 72'. This aircraft is sometimes illustrated with a plain white star on the fuselage, but close examination of this photo reveals it had the standard blue disc behind the star (*John Stanaway*)

Lt James Watkins shows the nose art on the starboard side of his P-40E's cowling. Watkins claimed just one victory in P-40s, but went on to add ten more kills after the 9th FS converted to the P-38. His last victory came on 2 April 1945 while he was serving a second combat tour in 49th FG headquarters (*Steve Ferguson*)

Lt Sidney Woods with his groundcrew, Sgt Amerlio and Sgt Pruitt, and their P-40E-1 41-25163 'White 74'. Woods flew throughout the Darwin campaign without success, but later scored two kills and a probable in P-38s over New Guinea. A second tour with the Eighth Air Force netted him five more victories in Mustangs (*John Stanaway*)

2Lt Robert G Oestreicher was leading a flight of five P-40s climbing for altitude when they were attacked from above by Zeros. Although caught at a disadvantage, Oestreicher was able to lead his flight into the attack, but the low and slow Warhawks were scattered and soon overwhelmed. Only Oestreicher managed to reach the safety of a nearby cloud as the others were shot down. A few moments later he emerged from the cloud cover and spotted two 'Vals' flying at 15,000 ft. He slipped behind them, shot one down in flames and scored hits on the other, which limped away trailing smoke.

Oestreicher had recorded the first of 79 confirmed victories which P-40 pilots would score in the skies over northern Australia.

The first Darwin attack, followed on 3 March by a strafing attack on the west coast port of Broome and the fall of Java three days later, stirred a wave of invasion panic throughout Australia. Operational training of the green pilots of the 49th PG, many of them recent graduates of flying school, was cut short so that they could be deployed to provide air defence. Fortunately, a cadre of 12 pilots just back from Java was available to provide experienced flight leaders for the three squadrons of the 49th. The 7th PS was sent to Horn Island, off the Queensland coast about 75 miles from New Guinea, on 4 March. The 8th PS went to Melbourne on 5 March, while the 9th PS made the long trek from New South Wales to Darwin, arriving at Batchelor Field on 18 March.

The 7th PS was the first to see action. When a formation of twin-engined Japanese G4M 'Betty' bombers, escorted by 12 Zeros, was reported heading toward Horn Island late in the morning of 14 March, the 7th PS scrambled all nine of its operational P-40Es. The Warhawk

Java veteran Capt Ben S Irvin, 9th FS CO for a short period in Darwin, leans against the wing of his P-40E (41-25164, 'White 75') *The Rebel*, showing the prominent Pegasus fuselage art. Irvin had two confirmed victories before returning to the US in September 1942 (*Steve Ferguson*)

formation, led by squadron commander Capt Robert Morrissey, became strung out during its climb to altitude and was unable to reach the enemy before the bombers had dumped their loads on the RAAF base at Horn Island. Reaching the enemy formation as it turned for home, Morrissey led 'A' Flight against the Zero escorts while 'B' Flight took on the bombers. During the combat that followed, Morrissey shot one Zero down to score the 'Forty-Niners' first victory of the war.

His wingman, future ace 2Lt A T House, also downed a Zero in his first pass, but then his guns jammed. When he spotted a Zero from the second element attacking Morrissey, House dived toward the enemy aircraft with useless guns, but managed to ram his right wing-tip into the canopy area of the Zero. House's P-40 whipped into a wild series of gyrations as the Zero fell from the sky, but he was able to regain control of the aircraft at 4000 ft and fly it back to Horn Island. It took House three attempts to land because the mangled wingtip caused it to roll each time he slowed down, but he eventually made it.

Another future ace who returned to Horn Island with a damaged aircraft was 2Lt Stephen Andrew. He would score one confirmed victory during his tour in the South Pacific, then add eight more victories over Europe flying P-51s with the 352nd FG, based in England.

The 7th PS claimed five victories in the 14 March combat for the loss of one P-40, but several other Warhawks were badly damaged in the scrap. With just seven operational fighters and six pilots left, Morrissey was ordered to pull his squadron back to the safety of Iron Range, about 200 miles south of Horn Island. From there, the squadron moved to Darwin in early April at about the same time that the 8th PS was released from its patrol duty over the capital city to reunite the group.

Meanwhile the 9th PS scored its first victory over Darwin on 22 March. 1Lt Stephen Poleschuk was in a flight of four P-40s sent up to search for a reported Japanese reconnaissance aircraft. He and his wingman, 2Lt Clyde Harvey, spotted the Ki-15 snooper and made several passes at it before shooting it down in flames into the sea west of Bathurst Island. On their return to base, the pilots flipped a coin to determine

Lt Clyde L Harvey Jr flew sharkmouthed Kittyhawk 'White 92' with the 9th FS/49th FG from Darwin in 1942. The aircraft still bears the RAF serial ET810 in black on the rear fuselage, and it appears to have a darker colour on the propeller spinner than its dark green/dark earth equivalent uppersurface camouflage. Harvey scored three victories during his combat tour (*Steve Ferguson*)

A former cavalry officer, Lt Bob Vaught flew with the 9th FS/49th FG throughout the defence of Darwin, and then moved with the unit to New Guinea in late 1942. He scored five confirmed victories, including three in P-40s, prior to being gravely wounded in a P-38 crash on 5 March 1943. He was invalided home to the US and did not return to combat (*John Stanaway*)

who would get credit for the kill, and Poleschuk won. It was his only confirmed victory of the war.

Combat encounters continued for the 9th PS on 28 and 31 March, but the first big engagement over Darwin came on 4 April 1942. On that day, an approaching Japanese force of six bombers, escorted by a similar number of Zeros, was spotted by radar at about 1300 hrs. Four P-40s were airborne on patrol at the time, led by 2Lt Grover Gardner, and a second flight of six led by Java veteran 2Lt Andrew Reynolds took off immediately. Gardner's flight struck first, making a head-on pass against the bombers and flaming one before engaging the Zeros. Within moments, Reynolds' flight followed Gardner into the bombers head-on and then joined the dogfight. Reynolds caught one Zero with a deflection shot and saw it fall

Ace Bob Vaught's P-40E 'White 94 *"BOB's ROBIN"* is seen sporting a gaudy sharkmouth as it sits under camouflage netting at Darwin in 1942. The name appeared on both sides of the fuselage, as did a flying skull cartoon just forward of the national insignia (*Steve Ferguson*)

All three of these 9th FS/49th FG pilots became aces. They are, from left to right, Lt John D Landers, Capt I B Jack Donalson and Capt Andrew Reynolds. Reynolds was the top-scoring USAAF ace in the Pacific, with 9.333 victories, between 30 July 1942 and 14 April 1943, when 1Lt Richard I Bong scored the tenth of his eventual 40 kills (*Steve Ferguson*)

Lt John Landers poses with the diving eagle artwork on his P-40E 'White 81' at Darwin. The bird was modelled on similar artwork displayed by Capt Andy Reynolds' P-40E 'White 86'. After scoring six victories in the Pacific, Landers went on to greater fame as a group commander in the Eighth Air Force, flying P-51s. His final score was 14.5 aerial victories (*Steve Ferguson*)

away from the flight. Outnumbered, the Zeros withdrew to regroup, allowing the Warhawk pilots to redirect their attention to the fleeing bombers. Reynolds had become separated from his flight and joined up with 2Lt John S Sauber to press an attack on three G4M 'Bettys' at 11,000 ft. Two of the big bombers fell toward the sea as the two P-40 pilots broke off due to low fuel supplies and a lack of ammunition.

While all this was going on, future ace 2Lt John D Landers of Reynolds' flight had been struggling to reach combat altitude because of a rough engine in his P-40. Landers eventually caught up with a trio of 'Bettys', one of which was already on fire, and downed two of them. None of the P-40s were shot down by enemy fire, but Gardner and his wingman, 2Lt J D Livingstone, were struck by a barrage of 'friendly' 40 mm anti-aircraft fire while returning to base. Gardner parachuted safely from his burning fighter, but Livingstone was killed when he crash-landed his P-40 at 34-Mile Field.

The 9th PS pilots were credited with nine victories on this day, although subsequent investigation suggested there was substantial double claiming. Be that as it may, Reynolds' two victories, added to one credited on 31 March and 3.33 scored in Java, made him the first pilot to reach ace status while flying with the 49th PG.

The next three weeks passed quietly before the Japanese attempted to strike another blow at Darwin, and its defending airfields. By this time, all three squadrons of the 49th PG would be ready and waiting for them. The attack came on Anzac Day, 25 April, celebrated as a holiday in Australia to commemorate the part its forces played in the Gallipoli campaign in 1915. Under the able leadership of Lt Col Paul Wurtsmith, the 49th put up 50 P-40s in the early afternoon to intercept enemy bombers detected by radar approaching from the former Allied base at Koepang, on Timor Island. One of the P-40 pilots was Java veteran Jim Morehead, leading the Yellow Flight of the 8th PS. He wrote this account of the action that ensued;

'Climbing offshore, my flight was to the east, with Capt (Mitchell) Sims' flight to the west. We were all moving past Melville Island, north of the mainland. We were approaching the service ceiling of the P-40, and I was offshore about 25 miles when I saw a large procession of enemy

29

Java veteran Lt James B Morehead used glossy red dots to mark his confirmed victories on P-40E-1 41-36171 'White 51' of the 8th FS/49th FG. He scored twice over Java, and added five more kills during the defence of Darwin, dating this photograph after 23 August 1942. Morehead claimed one more victory while flying P-38s in the Mediterranean theatre later in the war (*Steve Ferguson*)

bombers below us at about 16,000 ft. I had rarely seen their bombers below us before this. I called Capt Sims and asked if he wanted to make the attack, or should I. I was nearer the enemy formation than Capt Sims was, and it was logical that I make the attack. To my great relief, he said to go ahead. Recently, we had received a report of Japanese pilots doing aerobatics over Port Moresby, New Guinea, for the benefit of our airmen there. I decided to do the same for the benefit of the Japanese airmen assembled below, and to build confidence in my green troops who, as yet, had seen no combat. As I built up speed in a slight dive, I did a slow roll, and continued rolling into the attack on a quartering angle off the port bow. The Zeros were speeding to cut us off, but they were too late.

'I was approaching good range now. I led the lead bomber by about five ship-lengths, and with a little elevation I opened fire. My lead was exactly right as my tracers fed into the nose of the lead bomber. I held the trigger down all the way in on the pass until I had to pull off. The lead bomber appeared to be smoking from both engines. I then did a high-speed steep turn to the left, back into the formation. This was the one opportunity I had to charge into the Jap bombers at a decent altitude where the P-40 performed well. I blacked out in the turn but couldn't have timed it better. I came out on the tail of the last bomber, to within 50 yards of him.

'As my vision cleared, a dramatic scene unfolded before my eyes. My second element leader, Lt "Fip" Miller, and his wingman, Bill Herbert, had tacked onto an outside element of bombers and Miller was firing at a bomber. At that instant the right wing of the left-hand bomber broke off. The extra lift on the left wing spun the aircraft, the good wing struck the bomber next to it on the right, and they tangled together.

'I could observe no more as there were two healthy bombers right in front of me less than 70 yards away, and their gunners were firing at me. I cut my throttle and placed the gunsight on the nearest aeroplane and started firing. They all looked shiny new, and I knew we had not seen this aeroplane in the skies over Java. There were turrets right in the tail of the bomber, and I realised it was a 20 mm gun because it was firing so slowly. My tracers were going to the right of the gunner, who I could see plainly. I kicked left rudder, bringing the tracers right across the turret and the gunner stopped firing.

'I realised that the Zeros must be stacking up behind me on my tail, but it was now or never to be able to rip into those bombers. I pulled further to the left, raking the left engine, which started burning, but my speed was overtaking the big bomber, and I dived beneath it as I sped past. Now I was approaching the lead ship of this element, and his tail gunner was firing those slow shots at me. With my throttle back, and directly in the prop wash of both bombers, I was slowing rapidly. I glided right up to the

2Lt Rufus Jordan of the 8th FS/49th FG points to his name on the squadron readiness board in Darwin on 4 September 1942. Jordan claimed three confirmed victories and two probables between August 1942 and April 1943 (*Steve Ferguson*)

gunner and, precisely as before, I yawed the tracers across the turret and he stopped firing. I kept shooting, while switching to the right engine. About that time a sluice of oil came from the right engine of this last bomber, covering my windshield, then I stalled out, as I had forgotten to add throttle. I turned away from them as a Zero dived on me.'

Morehead diced with the Zero but failed to bring it down, then dived to safety when he felt the Zero pilot was getting the upper hand. Unknown to him, his P-40 had taken many hits in the engagement, and both tyres on the main landing gear were flat. The aircraft nosed up on landing, then fell back onto the landing gear, which collapsed. Morehead climbed out unhurt, now an ace with the three confirmed victories in the

2Lt Bill Hennon was another ace of the 17th Provisional PS in Java, scoring his fifth victory on 26 February 1942. Here, he poses with his 7th FS/49th FG P-40E 'White 36' in Australia in May 1942, several weeks before he recorded his final two kills. In the background is Lt Bob Vaught's *"BOB's ROBIN"* of the 9th FS (*Steve Ferguson*)

fight, giving him a total of five. He would score two more kills over Darwin before completing his tour, then add a final victory while flying P-38s in the Mediterranean theatre later in the war. The 8th PS was credited with a total of 11 kills in its first combat, and Capt Bill Hennon of the 7th PS got one Zero. Two days later, another raid would net six more victories for the 8th PS, one for the 7th PS and one for the 9th PS. Total losses for the 'Forty-Niners' during the two combats were four P-40s shot down, with two pilots killed and two wounded.

Six weeks would pass before the Japanese paid a return visit to hot, humid Darwin. In the interim, the enemy concentrated on attacking Allied units defending Port Moresby while the pilots of the 49th – its designation changed from 'pursuit' to 'fighter' group during this period – flew boring patrols, or sat sweating in their cockpits on alert. Four raids on Darwin between 13 and 16 June gave the 'Forty-Niners' 15 more victories for the loss of nine P-40s, but only one pilot killed.

The Japanese changed tactics in July, when they made a series of night raids of Darwin against which the P-40 pilots of the 49th FG were powerless. The next daylight raid on 30 July was a notable occasion for two 9th FS pilots. Blue Flight leader Andy Reynolds scored his final kill of the war, bringing his score to 9.333 confirmed, and making him the top-scoring ace in the Pacific theatre at that time. At the same time, Philippines veteran 1Lt I B Jack Donalson shot down a Zero to achieve his fifth victory, adding his name to the list of aces.

By this time, the Japanese were concentrating on their assault against Australian and American forces on New Guinea, so another three weeks passed before the next air raid against Darwin on 23 August. In this, the last interception over Darwin for the 49th FG, aces George Kiser and Jim Morehead scored their final victories of their Pacific tours. The total of 15 kills on the day brought the 49th FG's final tally during the defence of Darwin to 78 confirmed victories, eight probables and four damaged.

No longer a green outfit with just a sprinkling of combat veterans, the 49th was now a seasoned group ready to meet a new challenge. In September, with RAAF fighter squadrons now available to assume air defence duties at Darwin, the 49th FG began the next chapter in its remarkable history with a move to New Guinea.

Some fanciful artwork adorned the P-40Es of the 49th FG at Darwin. The 8th FS's 1Lt Randall D Keator had his 'White 68' marked with this pelican 'fighter-bomber' on one side and the name *The Spoddessape* on the other. Keator scored two victories in the Philippines in a P-40B on the first day of the war, then evacuated to Australia faster than a 'spotted-ass ape' (*Dwayne Tabatt*)

COLOUR PLATES

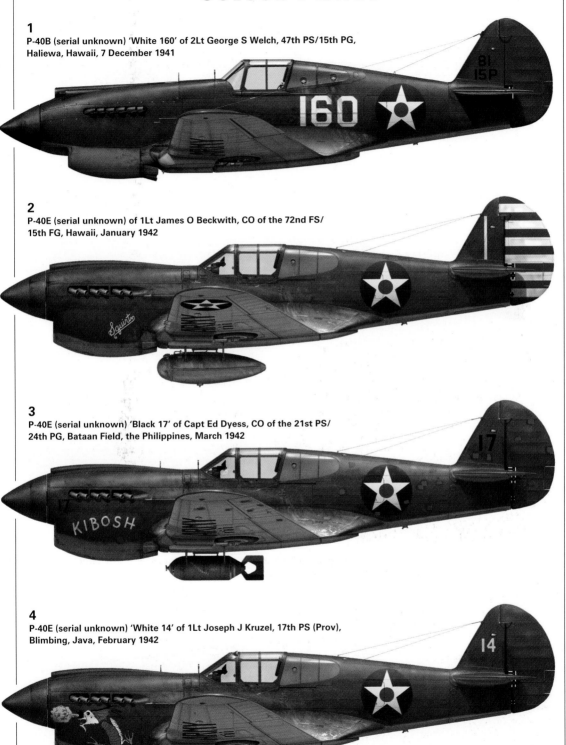

1
P-40B (serial unknown) 'White 160' of 2Lt George S Welch, 47th PS/15th PG,
Haliewa, Hawaii, 7 December 1941

2
P-40E (serial unknown) of 1Lt James O Beckwith, CO of the 72nd FS/
15th FG, Hawaii, January 1942

3
P-40E (serial unknown) 'Black 17' of Capt Ed Dyess, CO of the 21st PS/
24th PG, Bataan Field, the Philippines, March 1942

4
P-40E (serial unknown) 'White 14' of 1Lt Joseph J Kruzel, 17th PS (Prov),
Blimbing, Java, February 1942

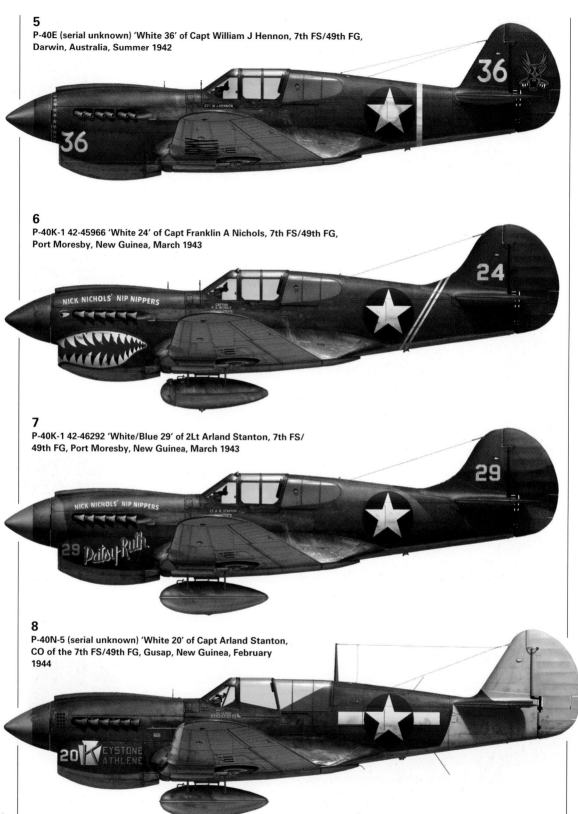

5
P-40E (serial unknown) 'White 36' of Capt William J Hennon, 7th FS/49th FG,
Darwin, Australia, Summer 1942

6
P-40K-1 42-45966 'White 24' of Capt Franklin A Nichols, 7th FS/49th FG,
Port Moresby, New Guinea, March 1943

7
P-40K-1 42-46292 'White/Blue 29' of 2Lt Arland Stanton, 7th FS/
49th FG, Port Moresby, New Guinea, March 1943

8
P-40N-5 (serial unknown) 'White 20' of Capt Arland Stanton,
CO of the 7th FS/49th FG, Gusap, New Guinea, February
1944

9
P-40N-5 (possibly 42-105405) 'White 13' of 1Lt Robert M DeHaven,
7th FS/49th FG, Gusap, New Guinea, late January 1944

10
P-40N-5 (serial unknown) 'White 24' of 1Lt Elliott E Dent Jr,
7th FS/49th FG, Gusap, New Guinea, late January 1944

11
P-40N-5 (serial unknown) 'White 7' of 1Lt Joel B Paris III, 7th
FS/49th FG, Hollandia, New Guinea, May 1944

12
P-40E-1 41-36171 'White 61' of 1Lt James B Morehead, 8th FS/49th FG,
Darwin, Australia, 25 April 1942

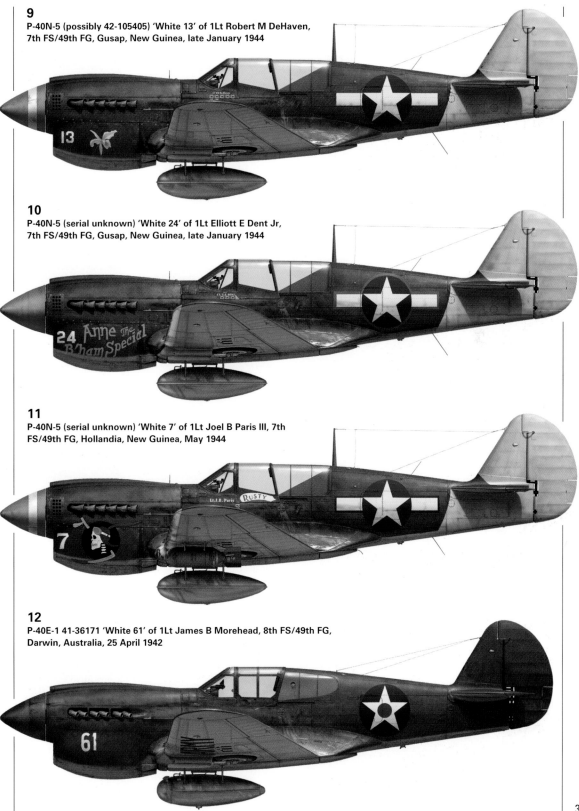

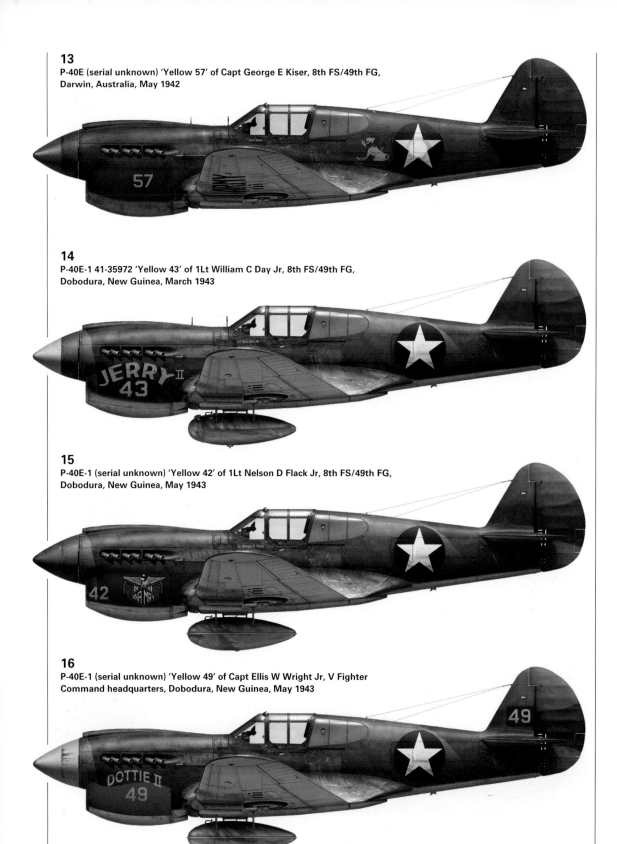

13
P-40E (serial unknown) 'Yellow 57' of Capt George E Kiser, 8th FS/49th FG,
Darwin, Australia, May 1942

14
P-40E-1 41-35972 'Yellow 43' of 1Lt William C Day Jr, 8th FS/49th FG,
Dobodura, New Guinea, March 1943

15
P-40E-1 (serial unknown) 'Yellow 42' of 1Lt Nelson D Flack Jr, 8th FS/49th FG,
Dobodura, New Guinea, May 1943

16
P-40E-1 (serial unknown) 'Yellow 49' of Capt Ellis W Wright Jr, V Fighter
Command headquarters, Dobodura, New Guinea, May 1943

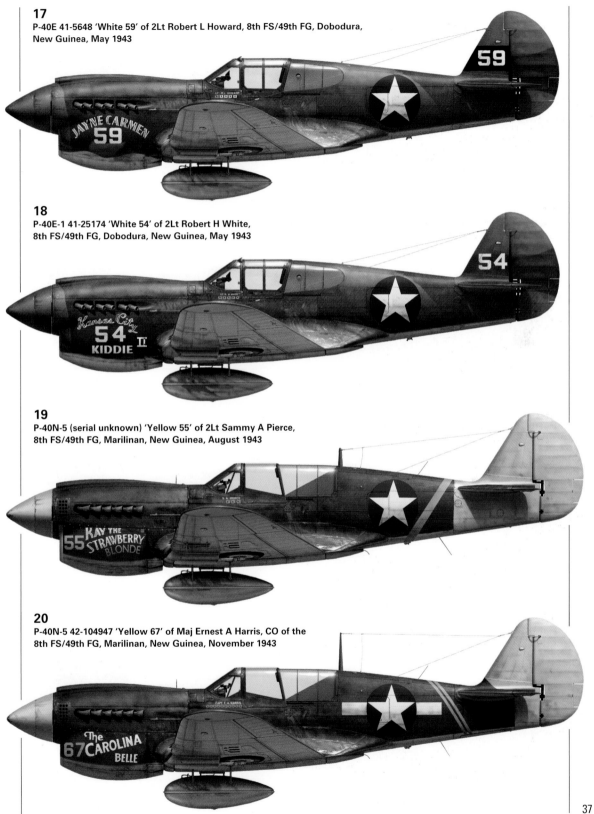

17
P-40E 41-5648 'White 59' of 2Lt Robert L Howard, 8th FS/49th FG, Dobodura,
New Guinea, May 1943

18
P-40E-1 41-25174 'White 54' of 2Lt Robert H White,
8th FS/49th FG, Dobodura, New Guinea, May 1943

19
P-40N-5 (serial unknown) 'Yellow 55' of 2Lt Sammy A Pierce,
8th FS/49th FG, Marilinan, New Guinea, August 1943

20
P-40N-5 42-104947 'Yellow 67' of Maj Ernest A Harris, CO of the
8th FS/49th FG, Marilinan, New Guinea, November 1943

21
P-40N-5 42-104990 'Yellow 42' of Capt Robert H White,
8th FS/49th FG, Marilinan, New Guinea, November 1943

22
P-40N-5 (serial unknown) 'Yellow 46' of 1Lt Robert W Aschenbrener,
8th FS/49th FG, Marilinan, New Guinea, December 1943

23
P-40N-5 42-105834 'Yellow 51' of 1Lt Donald W Meuten,
8th FS/49th FG, Gusap, New Guinea, April 1944

24
P-40E-1 41-24809 'White 83' of 2Lt I B Jack Donalson, 9th FS/49th FG,
Darwin, Australia, June 1942

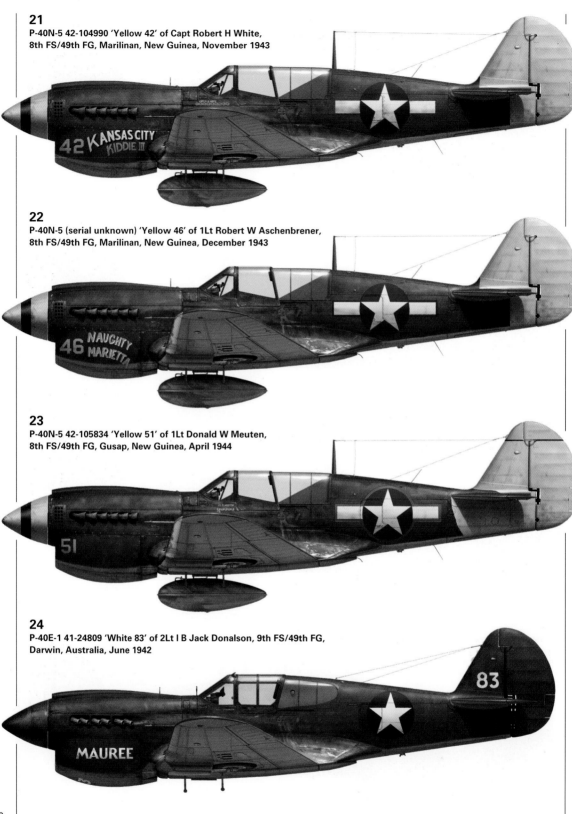

25
P-40E-1 (RAF serial probably ET503) 'White 86' of 1Lt Andrew J
Reynolds, 9th FS/49th FG, Darwin, Australia, July 1942

26
P-40E 41-5647 'White 81' of 2Lt John D Landers, 9th FS/49th FG,
Darwin, Australia, Summer 1942

27
P-40E-1 41-24872 'White 94' of 1Lt Robert H Vaught, 9th FS/49th FG,
Darwin, Australia, Summer 1942

28
P-40E 41-5316 'White 72' of 2Lt James A Watkins, 9th FS/49th FG,
Darwin, Australia, June 1942

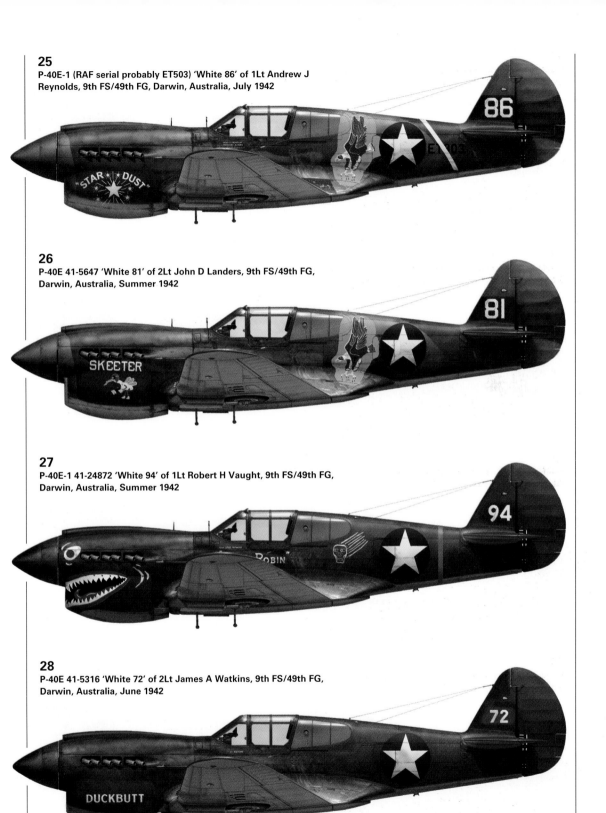

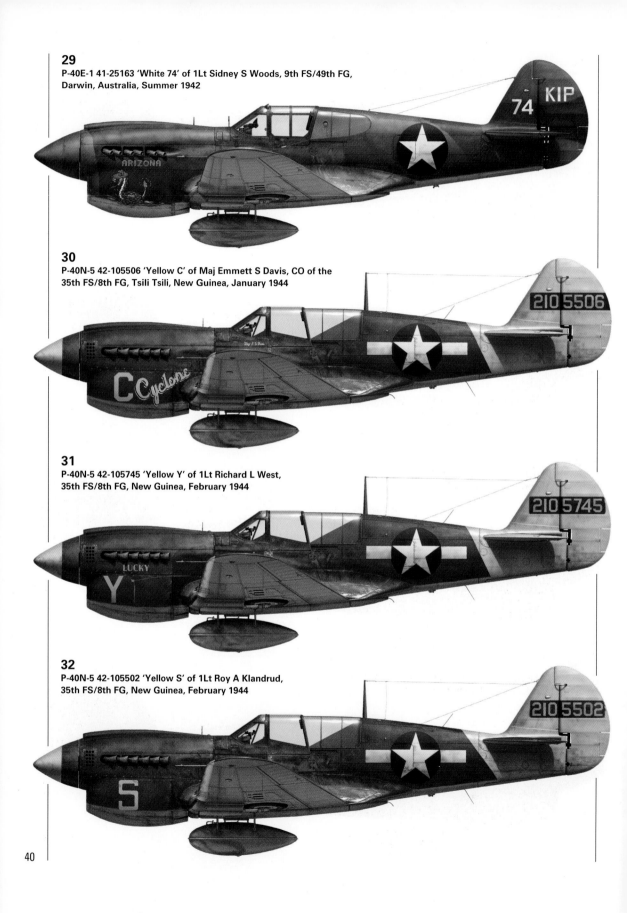

29
P-40E-1 41-25163 'White 74' of 1Lt Sidney S Woods, 9th FS/49th FG,
Darwin, Australia, Summer 1942

30
P-40N-5 42-105506 'Yellow C' of Maj Emmett S Davis, CO of the
35th FS/8th FG, Tsili Tsili, New Guinea, January 1944

31
P-40N-5 42-105745 'Yellow Y' of 1Lt Richard L West,
35th FS/8th FG, New Guinea, February 1944

32
P-40N-5 42-105502 'Yellow S' of 1Lt Roy A Klandrud,
35th FS/8th FG, New Guinea, February 1944

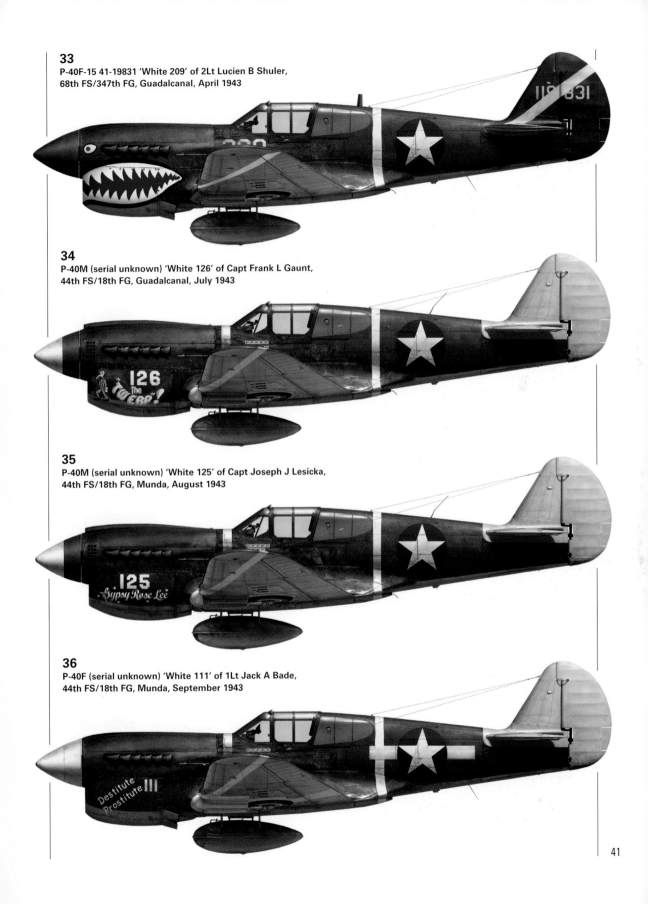

33
P-40F-15 41-19831 'White 209' of 2Lt Lucien B Shuler,
68th FS/347th FG, Guadalcanal, April 1943

34
P-40M (serial unknown) 'White 126' of Capt Frank L Gaunt,
44th FS/18th FG, Guadalcanal, July 1943

35
P-40M (serial unknown) 'White 125' of Capt Joseph J Lesicka,
44th FS/18th FG, Munda, August 1943

36
P-40F (serial unknown) 'White 111' of 1Lt Jack A Bade,
44th FS/18th FG, Munda, September 1943

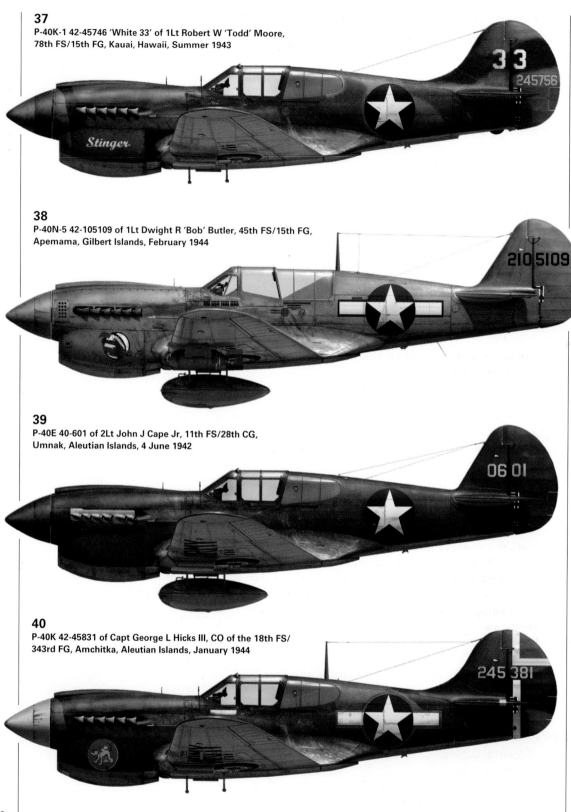

37
P-40K-1 42-45746 'White 33' of 1Lt Robert W 'Todd' Moore,
78th FS/15th FG, Kauai, Hawaii, Summer 1943

38
P-40N-5 42-105109 of 1Lt Dwight R 'Bob' Butler, 45th FS/15th FG,
Apemama, Gilbert Islands, February 1944

39
P-40E 40-601 of 2Lt John J Cape Jr, 11th FS/28th CG,
Umnak, Aleutian Islands, 4 June 1942

40
P-40K 42-45831 of Capt George L Hicks III, CO of the 18th FS/
343rd FG, Amchitka, Aleutian Islands, January 1944

THE NEW GUINEA CAMPAIGN

The Japanese invasion of New Guinea on 11 March 1942 opened a new phase of the Pacific war. The landings at Lae and Salamau on the north coast placed the key Allied harbour facilities at Port Moresby just one hour's flying time away for Japanese bombers. The port had to be held at all costs otherwise all of northern Australia would become vulnerable to invasion.

The only Allied fighter unit available to provide air defence for Port Moresby was the newly-formed No 75 Sqn RAAF, equipped with Kittyhawks (P-40Es supplied through Lend Lease). Although only four of its pilots had fighter combat experience, and many of them were fresh from training, the squadron deployed to Port Moresby on 17 March and went into action later that day. In a brilliantly-fought campaign, No 75 Sqn held Japanese raiders at bay for 44 days before American units, equipped with P-39 and P-400 Airacobras, arrived on 25 April to reinforce it.

The pressure on Port Moresby redoubled on 22 July 1942 when Japanese forces landed at Buna, directly across the Owen Stanley Range, on the north coast of New Guinea. From there, Japanese troops threatened both Port Moresby and also the new airfields at Milne Bay, on the eastern tip of New Guinea. Although Australian ground forces were able to drive the Japanese back from Milne Bay, another Japanese force in the mountains reached Imita Range, just 20 miles inland from Port Moresby, by mid-September.

With the fight for Port Moresby approaching its climax, the 7th FS/49th FG was ordered up from Darwin to contribute its P-40s to the Allied forces in New Guinea. Under the command of Capt Bill Hennon, the 7th FS arrived at 14-mile Drome, outside Port Moresby, on 14 September, and immediately began flying fighter-bomber missions in support of the Australian troops fighting along the Kokoda Trail. These missions, which included strafing, dive-bombing and escort duties, were very effective at helping the Australians halt the enemy advance. By the end of the month the Japanese were retreating northward toward Buna.

While this action was underway, the 8th FS had withdrawn from Darwin to repair and overhaul its well-worn P-40Es at Townsville, while the 9th FS remained at Darwin to help train the RAAF squadrons which were taking over air-defence duties there. The 9th FS was intended to be re-equipped with high-performance P-38s as soon as they became available, although it continued to fly some P-40s in the meantime. Soon both squadrons and 49th FG headquarters joined the 7th FS at airfields around Port Moresby.

Late October saw the first P-40Ks arrive in New Guinea. This model was similar to the P-40E, but featured an uprated Allison engine and a modified vertical stabiliser to help handle the extra power. The new aircraft, which were concentrated in the 7th FS, boasted slightly better climb performance and speed in level flight, although their service ceiling was no better than that of the P-40E. Yet they would prove outstanding in the fighter-bomber role, and at least as capable as the P-40E in air-to-air combat. But more important to the pilots of the 7th FS was that the P-40Ks were new.

——— EARLY ACTION OVER NEW GUINEA ———

The 49th FG got its first crack at Japanese aircraft over New Guinea during a sharp engagement on 1 November 1942. Eight P-40Es of the 8th FS, which had only arrived at Three-Mile Strip the previous week, were escorting A-20s near the enemy stronghold at Lae when four of them were jumped by A6M Zeros on the return flight to Port Moresby. Immediately, the No 4 Warhawk, flown by 2Lt Glenn Wohfford, was shot down. But flight leader 1Lt Dick Dennis and his wingman, 1Lt Bill Day, managed to turn into the attacking Zeros.

Dennis struck first, firing into a Zero which snap-rolled into an inverted spin and fell into the jungle. Then Day, a 22-year-old from Pennsylvania who had flown with the 8th FS throughout the Darwin campaign, blasted a Zero in a head-on pass and saw it fall in flames. It was the first of five confirmed victories for Day. His last victory, scored on 11 March 1943, made him the first P-40 pilot in the 49th FG to score five kills over New Guinea. Dick Dennis was posted missing in action about six weeks after the 1 November mission.

The 7th FS had its first encounter with Japanese aircraft over New Guinea on 22 November, scoring two victories and three probables for the loss of two P-40s with one pilot killed. The squadron fared somewhat better on 30 November in a fracas over the enemy garrison at Buna. With 1Lt Frank Nichols leading, 16 P-40s of the 7th FS were providing escort to eight bomb-carrying Warhawks of the 8th FS when a swarm of Zeros pounced on Green Flight out of nearby cloud. Two P-40s went down immediately and both pilots were killed before Nichols led his Red Flight into the scrap.

By using mutually supportive manoeuvres, all four members of Nichols' flight, plus Lt Don Lee of Green Flight, were able to claim victories. Besides Nichols, who would reach ace status after transferring to the P-38-equipped 475th FG in 1943, future ace 2Lt Arland Stanton scored his first victory on 30 November. He would go on to fly with the 7th FS well into 1944, eventually assuming command of the squadron and running up a score of eight confirmed victories.

The 9th FS got its first taste of aerial combat over New Guinea on 7 December 1942 – the first anniversary of the Pearl Harbor attack. Again, the action took place over Buna, where Allied efforts to eject the entrenched Japanese troops

Replacement pilot and ace Lt William C Day Jr flew P-40E 'Yellow 43' in the 8th FS/49th FG. He recorded five victories in the opening three months of 1943 to become the first 'all-New Guinea' ace of the 49th FG. The aircraft carried the name *Jerry* on the port side of the nose and *Mary-Willie* on the starboard, barely visible in this picture. The fighter's wheel centres are decorated with four yellow bomb markers (*Steve Ferguson*)

were reaching their climax. In a last-ditch attempt to assist the besieged garrison, the Japanese sent a formation of twin-engined bombers, with heavy Zero escort, from Rabaul to attack Allied ground positions. First to reach the raiders was a 7th FS flight, which attacked the bombers head-on before they reached landfall. Again it was led by Frank Nichols, who shot down one of two bombers to fall after the initial pass. The bombers dropped their loads harmlessly into the sea and turned homewards, but they ran smack into a patrol flight of eight 9th FS Warhawks led by Java and Darwin veteran 1Lt Bob Vaught.

Using Darwin-tested dive-and-zoom tactics, Vaught knocked down two bombers in his sharkmouthed P-40E *BOB'S ROBIN* for his second and third victories. Two other pilots in his flight scored kills before the Zero escorts intervened and the P-40 pilots broke off to return to Port Moresby unscathed. The last Japanese troops evacuated Buna a week later, and the Allies' difficult westward campaign along the north coast of New Guinea was underway.

The 49th FG's last encounters of 1942 marked a major change in the air war over New Guinea. Enemy positions at Lae were the next obvious objective for the Allied ground campaign, and the Japanese responded by bolstering their air defences with the addition of an army fighter unit, the 11th *Sentai*, equipped with Ki-43 'Oscars'. Combat-tested in China and South-east Asia, the 11th, was considered to be the most capable Japanese Army Air Force fighter unit at the time. Its Ki-43s, although lightly armed and not particularly fast, were probably the most manoeuvrable aircraft in New Guinea – certainly capable of giving a P-40 pilot trouble if he allowed himself to be drawn into a turning fight.

On 26 December, following a lull in operations caused by bad weather, the 11th *Sentai* sent a formation of Ki-43s to strafe the new Allied airstrip at Dobodura, just inland from Buna. The 'Oscars' caught a flight of RAAF Hudson transports attempting to land at Dobodura, but a dozen 9th FS Warhawks led by 1Lt John D Landers were patrolling nearby and hurried to the rescue. Diving through broken clouds, the P-40s tore into the Ki-43 and a swirling dogfight began, raging from 5000 ft down to tree-top level. Futures aces 1Lt Jim Watkins and 2Lt Art Wenige were two of the five P-40 pilots who claimed single victories.

Landers became separated from his flight during the diving attack and found himself single-handedly attacking six 'Oscars'. His only choice was to engage in a display of wild aerobatics, during which he was able to knock down two enemy fighters. Eventually, however, an 'Oscar' latched onto his tail and would not let go. The Warhawk took several bursts of accurate machine gun fire as Landers attempted to dive out of the fight, but his aircraft was doomed. He baled out at 1000 ft and landed in the jungle, where he was befriended by natives who were amazed by the appearance of the tall, blonde pilot from Oklahoma.

Landers returned to Four-Mile strip at Port Moresby the following day to learn that one of his two kills had been declared the 49th FG's 100th confirmed victory. His total now stood at six, making him the first pilot in the 49th to become an ace in New Guinea, and the first 'all 49th' ace. After his tour in the South Pacific, Landers returned to action flying P-38s and P-51s over Europe with the Eighth Air Force. His final tally was 14.5 confirmed aerial victories, one damaged and 20 strafing kills.

Much-travelled 2Lt George Chandler flew this P-40E with the 8th FS/49th FG during February and March 1943. He soon transferred to the 339th FS/ 347th FG at Guadalcanal, where he scored five confirmed victories (*Dwayne Tabatt*)

— THE LONG PUSH —

As 1943 opened, the 9th FS completed its re-equipment with P-38s, leaving the 7th and 8th FSs as the only USAAF P-40 units in New Guinea. Though small in number, the Warhawk force still packed a punch, as the 8th FS amply demonstrated on 7 January 1943.

With Allied forces putting increasing pressure on Lae, the Japanese high command decided in early January 1943 to reinforce the embattled garrison. At Rabaul, New Britain, Japanese troops recently diverted from Guadalcanal boarded five merchant ships for the 600-mile trip down the south coast of New Britain and across the Huon Gulf to Lae. Coast watchers on New Britain spotted the convoy on 6 January and radioed the alarm to Port Moresby, where the Fifth Air Force ordered an immediate search-and-destroy mission by heavy bombers, escorted by P-38s. The convoy survived, but by the next morning it had advanced to within range of bomb-carrying P-40s at Port Moresby.

The first mission force of the day comprised two flights of 7th FS P-40Ks, each carrying two 300-lb bombs and a centreline drop tank, covered by three more flights of 7th FS P-40s, with P-38s flying high cover. They found the convoy 40 miles offshore from the isthmus at Salamaua just as escorting Ki-43 'Oscars' attacked the top-cover P-40s. A sharp engagement ensued in which the Warhawk pilots claimed two probables and two damaged while the assault flights dived to attack the enemy ships.

Hampered by clouds, heavy flak and their own inexperience in dive-bombing moving targets, the Warhawks managed just a single hit on the ships when one of Lt Claude Burtnette's '300 pounders' hit the *Myoko Maru* amidships. Despite heavy damage to its engine room, the ship managed to limp on toward Lae. All aircraft of the 7th FS returned safely.

Learning that the convoy was continuing toward Lae, the Port Moresby command ordered a second strike. Four flights of P-40Es from the 8th FS got the job and took off in the late afternoon with orders to strafe the convoy. Led by 1Lt Ernest A Harris, the Warhawks found the ships just offshore from Lae village. They were attacked immediately by Ki-43s of the 11th *Sentai* and A6M 'Hamps' of the 582nd *Kotukai*, and only Harris was able to complete a strafing pass against the ships. In the fierce dogfight that ensued, three futures aces of the 8th FS scored their first victories as the squadron claimed 13 confirmed, two probables and two damaged. This is Harris's account;

'I was leading a flight of four aeroplanes. Before reaching the target we were attacked by Zeros. My flight split up and engaged the enemy. I continued on and strafed one transport. I observed pieces flying from the deck of the ship but was unable to observe other damage. I pulled up into the fight and attacked a Zero that was on the tail of a P-40. I closed in on him, shooting, and saw him burst into flames. I pulled up and made a pass at a second Zero and put three long bursts into him and observed the bullets striking the aeroplane and pieces disintegrating from it. The aeroplane rolled over out of control and into a layer of cloud. I immediately pulled up and made a pass at a third Zero. I pressed the attack to a very close range and fired two bursts into him and saw my bullets striking him in the cockpit. The Zero began spiralling down, seemingly out of control, into the clouds. I dived, circling the clouds and getting under them. I observed the aeroplane burning on the water, and two other large circular wakes where aeroplanes had hit the water. These were all in the vicinity of where Zeros I had attacked had gone through the clouds.'

1Lt Robert H White of the 8th FS/ 49th FG was already an ace when he shot down two 'Betty' bombers and a 'Tony' fighter over Wewak on 6 September 1943. Here, he climbs down from his P-40N 'White 42' *Kansas City KIDDIE III* at Marilinan after claiming his ninth, and final, victory on 11 November 1943 (*Dwayne Tabatt*)

Harris was credited with three victories. The man from Tennessee, who was highly regarded for his flying skills and leadership ability, would become CO of the 8th FS later in 1943 and go on to set the standard for P-40 pilots in the Pacific with ten confirmed victories. He was later killed in an F-80 crash while serving in Germany in 1949.

The two other future aces of the 8th FS who opened their scoring on 7 January were 2Lts Robert H White, with two victories, and Robert L Howard, with one confirmed and one probable. One P-40 was shot down in the fight.

The assault on Lae continued through the spring and summer of 1943, with the Warhawks of the 49th FG right in the middle of the action. Although the decisive Battle of the Bismarck Sea (1 to 3 March) effectively sealed Lae's fate when the Fifth Air Force wiped out another Japanese relief convoy attempting to reach the stronghold, the defenders would hold on until mid-September. Warhawks were not involved in the Bismarck Sea action, which took place beyond their effective range.

One of just seven Americans to earn ace status in two wars, 1Lt James P Hagerstrom scored six victories over New Guinea with the 8th FS/49th FG. His best day was 23 January 1944 when he shot down three 'Hamps' and a 'Tony 'over Wewak. He added eight victories to his score in the Korean War, flying F-86s with the 4th FIW (*John Stanaway*)

The 49th FG completed a move to the new airfield complex at Dobodura in early March. Now the P-40s were just 175 miles from Lae, and they were even closer to the harbour at Salamaua, which was another regular entry on their target list. The Japanese response was not long in arriving. Bombers from Rabaul raided Dobodura, and the nearby harbour at Oro Bay, resulting in four victory claims by the 8th FS on 11 March and seven more on the 28th.

Meanwhile, the 7th FS had to content itself with patrols and dive-bombing missions near Salamaua. Action resumed on 11 April, and the 7th FS became involved in air combat for the first time in more than a month when the Japanese opened a renewed assault from Rabaul, called Operation *I-GO*, against targets in New Guinea. Scrambling a few minutes before noon, Warhawks of the 7th and 8th FSs proceeded north over Oro Bay to intercept a large formation of enemy aircraft already under attack from patrolling P-38s. Two 'Val' dive-bombers were shot down by the 7th FS and the 8th FS claimed seven victories. Three of the 8th's kills were credited to Ernie Harris, taking his total to seven, and

The starboard side cowling of Flt Off Sammy A Pierce's P-40E 41-36246 'Yellow 42' of the 8th FS carried the name *Pistoff Pat*. This was his first Warhawk, and he used it to claim his first victory on 11 April 1943 (*Dwayne Tabatt*)

The name *KAY – STRAWBERRY BLONDE* appeared on the port side of Flt Off Pierce's 'Yellow 42', shown here at Dobodura in the spring of 1943. Its worn appearance is typical of 49th FG Warhawks during this period (*Dwayne Tabatt*)

making him an ace. Future aces 2Lt James P Hagerstrom and Flt Off Sammy A Pierce also scored their first confirmed victories. The 8th FS repeated its success the following day in a late morning interception off Cape Ward Hunt, when five more victories were scored.

The Warhawks' next aerial encounter would turn out to be their biggest success of the entire New Guinea campaign. On 14 May the Japanese again attempted to bomb the complex of bases at Dobodura and dock facilities at Oro Bay, and again the defenders responded with a harsh greeting. A force of 18 'Betty' bombers, with 32 escorting Zeros approaching from Rabaul over the Solomon Sea, found all three squadrons of the 49th FG ready and waiting for them. P-38s of the 9th FS struck first, but the Warhawk pilots did most of the scoring as the 7th FS notched up five victories and the 8th was credited with an impressive 13. Pierce was in the last flight of 8th FS P-40s to scramble for the interception, led by the ever-aggressive Harris, and he reported;

'Our flight climbed to the right-hand side above the bomber formation. The flight leader rolled into a 180-degree overhead pass, picking out the first ship in the first element of the bomber formation. I followed him in, picking up the lead ship in the second element of the Jap formation. I was firing from a position of relatively straight down, and my windshield began to fog. I tried to clear it off, and as a consequence my pull-out was a little late. I damned near rammed the Jap wingman in the outside element of the formation. I cleaned my windshield of fog and moisture.

'While rejoining, I spotted a Jap fighter making a pass on the number three man in our flight (2Lt Bob Howard). The Jap was slightly above and 45-degrees to my right. I pulled the nose far enough in front of his line of flight to at least shoot in front of him. It was all I could do to take him off the No 3 man. When I fired, I saw hits on the "Zeke" around the wing root and just forward of the wing on the fuselage. He fell off to the left in a steep diving attitude. I followed him and fired one more burst into him until he hit the water.

'Climbing back up, I found I'd been separated from the flight leader and the number three man. I climbed above the bombers, which by this time had jettisoned their bombs and were high-tailing it for New Britain. I made my first pass on the third element of the bombers and knocked out one engine of a bomber, which lost altitude. As he dropped I made three more passes at him until I ran out of ammo. Now the "Zekes" were on me. A three-ship element came down after me. It was my turn to run. Heading for home and putting my nose down, I managed to outrun my three pursuers.'

Pierce was credited with one Zero and one 'Betty' destroyed. Howard got two victories and White one, both adding their names to the 8th's roster of aces. All three men would add to their scores, Howard finishing the war with six victories, Pierce with seven and White with nine, including a triple kill on 6 September 1943.

As the summer of 1943 arrived, the P-40Es, E-1s and Ks were definitely showing their age, despite the groundcrews' heroic efforts to keep them flying. Those of the 49th FG merited much of the credit for the their squadron's successes. They had to endure all of the hardships of life on a jungle airstrip, including heat, humidity, boredom, bad food and a variety of unpleasant insects such as malaria-carrying mosquitoes, not to mention occasional enemy bombing raids. But unlike the pilots, who knew they would be rotating home at the completion of a certain number of missions, ground personnel could see not see any end to their gruelling life in the jungle.

The P-38 squadrons of V Fighter Command dominated air combat over New Guinea during July and August 1943. The 7th FS completed its scoring in the P-40K with two July engagements in which its pilots scored nine victories. Notable

The 49th FG received new P-40N-5s in the summer of 1943, and 2Lt Sammy Pierce, seen here in his favourite baseball cap, was allotted 'Yellow 55'. Note the hand crank sticking out of the cowling to the left of Pierce. This was used to start the engine, as electric starters were omitted from early P-40Ns to save weight (*Dwayne Tabatt*)

1Lt Richard J Vodra of the 8th FS/49th FG decorated the rudder of his P-40N 'Yellow 41' with black checks in the autumn of 1943 at Marilinan. Vodra was responsible for obtaining a Disney cartoon of a 'black sheep' which became the 8th FS mascot, and gave the squadron its nickname. Examining the paint job are, from left to right, Capt Dan W Moore, Capt Clyde H Barnett Jr and 1Lt Harry J McCullough (*Steve Ferguson*)

among them were the first successes of future aces Elliott E Dent Jr and Robert M DeHaven.

The old Warhawks had done a great job over New Guinea during 1943. From the beginning of the year until their last engagement on 14 July, the 7th and 8th FSs had accounted for 87 Japanese aircraft destroyed at a cost of just five pilots killed in action or in operational accidents. Then word reached the squadrons that they would be getting new aircraft.

The pilots had been hoping for P-38s but this was not to be. A shipment of 90 P-40N-5s – the latest model of Warhawk – had reached Australia and were intended to replace the old ones. The new Warhawk brought a slight improvement over previous models, featuring a slightly more powerful engine and an improved cockpit canopy system which gave the pilot better visibility. Efforts had been made to reduce weight in the airframe as well, giving the aircraft an improved rate of climb and top speed, but its combat ceiling remained well below those of contemporary fighters, both friend and foe.

The purple orchid nose art on P-40N-5 'White 13' identifies it as the Warhawk assigned to 1Lt Robert M DeHaven of the 7th FS/49th FG in January 1944. DeHaven believed 13 was his lucky number because his birthday was 13 January (*Steve Ferguson*)

DeHaven's old P-40N 'White 13' was rebuilt at Gusap in February-March 1944 and then reassigned to the 8th FS/49th FG as 'Yellow 67'. The name *Rita* on the starboard cowling (together with the seven kill flags on the port side of the fuselage) was carried over from DeHaven's days, but the yellow number and yellow/black/yellow spinner are 8th FS markings (*Steve Ferguson*)

─────── 'CYCLONE'S FLYING CIRCUS' ───────

The arrival of P-40Ns may have been disappointing for the 7th and 8th FS pilots, but a third unit re-equipping with the new model was more enthusiastic. To the 35th FS/8th FG, which had been flying P-39 Airacobras in New Guinea for more than a year, almost any new fighter represented an improvement. The squadron had been credited with just 23 confirmed victories since April 1942, and had scored only one

Maj E S 'Cyclone' Davis leads his 35th FS/8th FG on a flight to Tsili Tsili, New Guinea, in their new P-40Ns in September 1943. Davis is flying 42-105506 'Yellow C'. Note how the serial numbers on 35th FS P-40Ns were masked over when the white tail marking was applied, unlike those of the 49th FG (*Emmett S Davis*)

kill in the first six months of 1943. Summer 1943 found the 35th FS at Port Moresby under the command of Maj 'Cyclone' Davis, the pre-eminent dogfighter of pre-war Wheeler Field. Davis and his pilots were extremely frustrated by their Airacobras' short range and poor performance, and when Davis learned that enough P-40Ns were available to equip a third squadron, he jumped at the chance to have them for the 35th FS. It would prove to be a wise move.

The capture of Lae and Salamaua in mid-September brought new opportunities for the Warhawk pilots of V Fighter Command. Japanese aerial forces pulled back 300 miles up the New Guinea coast to Wewak, while Allied engineers immediately commenced work on the building of new airfields at Nadzab in the Markham Valley, inland from Lae.

The 8th FS had given the P-40N its first taste of aerial combat on 6 September when a four-aircraft patrol led by 1Lt Bob White shot down three 'Betty' bombers and a Ki-61 'Tony' fighter near Lae. Davis led 18 P-40Ns of the 35th FS to the new airfield at Tsili Tsili on 21 September 1943, and from then on the squadron that called itself 'Cyclone's Flying Circus' would begin living up to its name.

Tsili Tsili, one of the Nadzab fields, was just 90 miles from Finschafen, where the Allies were preparing for a sea-borne invasion. From there, the 35th FS could mount standing patrols over the invasion fleet.

The action started immediately with a successful interception on 22 September. One of the 35th FS pilots to see combat on that day was 1Lt Roy A Klandrud, who reported;

1Lt William C 'Willie' Drier barely escaped being shot down by P-38s of the 9th FS during the big scrap over Wewak on 6 September 1943 when the Lightning pilots mistook his P-40N 'Yellow 60' *Little MAGGIE* for a Ki-61 'Tony'. He later scored six victories while flying P-38s and rose to command the 49th FG's 8th FS (*Dwayne Tabatt*)

Pilots of the 35th FS/8th FG pose at Dobodura, New Guinea, in October 1943. Between September 1943 and February 1944, while 'Cyclone's Flying Circus' was equipped with P-40Ns, the 35th FS was credited with 65 confirmed victories (*John Stanaway*)

1Lt Glen 'Gabby' Holder of the 35th FS/8th FG poses in his P-40N-5 ('Yellow L' 42-105288) at Cape Gloucester, New Britain, in February 1944. Holder scored two victories in his squadron's record-setting scrap over Saidor, New Guinea, on 16 January 1944, when the 35th was credited with 19 victories and no losses. One of Holder's victims that day was a Ki-61 'Tony' flown by 14-kill ace WO Takashi Noguchi of the 68th *Sentai*, JAAF (*John Holder*)

'The enemy was approaching our Navy convoy in the Huon Gulf off Finschafen, some coming in low with a top cover of fighters. I sighted one Zero on a straight course. The wingman pulled up into a vertical roll. I challenged this with a chandelle to the left, maintaining visual contact. The pilot made his fatal mistake by levelling out with his tail directly away, whereas I squeezed off and paddled my rudder, causing a spray of ammo which disfigured a total kill. This victory was witnessed by Lt Glen Holder.'

The 35th's total score for the day was seven confirmed victories and two probables. Klandrud would score twice more in the course of completing 196 missions during his 22-month overseas tour. Another 35th FS pilot scoring for the first time on 22 September was 2Lt Richard L West, who claimed two 'Hamps' destroyed and one probable. The young man from Missouri was a former tactical instructor whose flying skills and self-confidence were said to rival those of his squadron commander. He would put them to good use, claiming six victories in P-40s and eight more after the 35th FS was re-equipped with P-38s, ending the war as the squadron's top scorer.

The 35th FS was back in action on 27 September, this time escorting B-24s to Wewak after topping up their fuel tanks at advanced airstrip Bena Bena. Davis, who led the mission, recalled;

'After refuelling our aeroplanes, we sat in our cockpits to await the arrival of the bombers. A sergeant with binoculars sighted the bombers above the horizon. The aircraft were started and we took off in pairs. The 16 of us intercepted the bombers and escorted them on their mission. There were 12 B-24s in the formation. We positioned our fighters behind and above the bombers so we could check their "six o'clock" position. Our fighter aeroplanes flew in a spread finger-tip formation. Each flight of four was separated by about 2000 ft. With the flights being in a line-abreast formation, we could pretty well "check six" on each other.

'A couple of P-38 squadrons had been on fighter sweeps earlier that morning and had flushed up all of the enemy's available fighters and run them out of petrol, because when the B-24s made their bomb runs no enemy fighters showed up to challenge them. The bombers withdrew to the south. Their flight altitude was about 16,000 ft. Our P-40Ns were about 1000 ft above and behind them. There was an overcast sky about 1000 ft above us.

'As we cruised along at 17,000 ft, two enemy fighters appeared out of the overcast. They were about 3000 ft behind Blue Flight on my left. A pilot in my flight was "checking six". I heard the radio call "Blue flight, bogies at 'six o'clock'". A pilot by the name of Bacchus B Byrd was the fourth man in blue flight. He looked behind him, saw the enemy aeroplanes, and rolled upside down to the right, then put his fighter in a vertical dive toward the jungle below. The first enemy aeroplane dived after Byrd's P-40. I did a sharp left diving turn toward the two diving aircraft at full throttle. I could see the P-40 pulling away from the enemy aeroplane, which was a Ki-61 "Tony". The "Tony" had a liquid-cooled engine like a P-40, and we thought it was a copy of an Italian fighter.

'As we dived toward the ground, I could see that the P-40 had successfully escaped. The Japanese pilot, realising that the chase was futile, pulled up into a 45-degree climb. I was above and behind him, so this was all to my advantage. I manoeuvred my P-40 behind and slightly to the left of the "Tony". I put my gunsight pipper just in front of the enemy aeroplane and squeezed the trigger on my control stick. I only fired about a three-second burst. I saw bullets hit the left wing root of the "Tony", but nothing spectacular happened. So I fired another two-second burst and the Tony exploded. I turned my P-40 to the right and as I looked down I saw another P-40 in hot pursuit of the other enemy aircraft. A moment

Maj E S 'Cyclone' Davis, CO of the 35th FS/8th FG, lent his nickname to his P-40N-5, as well as to his squadron. Davis, considered a master dogfighter, was officially credited with three confirmed victories, but his actual total was probably higher. He commanded the 8th FG between January and June 1944 and again from June to December 1945 (*John Stanaway*)

1Lt Richard L West poses with his P-40N-5 'Yellow Y' (42-105745) after his sixth confirmed victory on 15 November 1943, making him the first ace of the 35th FS/8th FG. The aggressive ace from Missouri, one of the few P-40 pilots who could stay with 'Cyclone' Davis in the air, took his score to 14 confirmed victories after the 35th FS converted to P-38s. On the ground, Dick West stood out thanks to his long hair, which he refused to cut after his first engagement with enemy aircraft two months prior to 'making ace'. US press releases following his November successes called him the 'Sampson of the South Pacific' (*John Stanaway*)

later that P-40 pilot, Capt Don Thomas, fired his guns and the enemy aeroplane exploded. The 35th FS pilots joined up in formation again, and I led them back to the Tsili Tsili airstrip.'

The 35th FS continued to build its reputation as a 'hot' outfit in a series of successful combats over the next few months. On 15 November, Dick West became the first ace of the 35th when he shot down two 'Zekes' and two 'Sallys' to bring his score to six confirmed. Then, on 26 December, the squadron bagged 18 victories in its best day yet. 'Cyclone' Davis believed he shot down five or six enemy aircraft that day, but the combination of losing his wingman and a defective gun camera resulted in his receiving confirmation for just two victories. This would prove significant, as shortly afterwards he was promoted to command the 8th FG, and he never got another chance to add to his official score of three confirmed victories.

The 35th FS's last aerial combat in the P-40N turned out to be its most successful. On 2 January 1944, the Allies landed at Saidor, the next stop on the march up New Guinea's north coast. Over the next two weeks positions were secured as convoys of merchant ships brought additional troops and equipment. By 16 January, most of the aerial activity had shifted eastward to New Britain and westward to Wewak. The pilots of the 35th FS were not expecting much action when 15 of them commenced a patrol over Saidor that morning, but after about an hour of circling over the convoy they spotted a large formation of Japanese fighters approaching from the direction of Wewak.

One of the P-40N pilots involved in the action that day was 1Lt William A Gardner, a New Englander who had been employed designing aircraft engines for the Curtiss-Wright corporation before the war. He was flying as an element leader, with 2Lt Kenneth R 'Bud' Pool on his wing. Gardner wrote this account for a V Fighter Command publication later in the war;

'My first contacts with the enemy were in the latter part of 1943. The Jap fighter formations were loose and could be recognised in the distance as a swarm of flies. Many of the aeroplanes would flip momentarily on their backs for a good look underneath while others would be rolling. In early 1944 there seemed to be a change in their air tactics. Their

1Lt Dick West's P-40N, shown here with its groundcrew, had the name *LUCKY* painted on its engine cowling in early 1944 (*John Stanaway*)

Future ace Lt K R 'Bud' Pool of the 35th FS/8th FG poses with P-40N 'Yellow F'. Pool, then a junior member of the squadron, did not have a personal aircraft until the unit converted to P-38s. After scoring his first two victories in a P-40N during the big battle of 16 January 1944, Pool added three more kills in P-38s later that year (*John Stanaway*)

1Lt Lynn E Witt Jr (right) and crew chief S/Sgt Gordon E Hoover show off their scoreboard after Witt's fourth victory with the 35th FS/ 8th FG on 16 January 1944. The aircraft was probably 'Yellow J'. Witt, who had originally earned his wings as a sergeant pilot, added two victories in P-38s to bring his final score to six (*John Stanaway*)

1Lt William A Gardner (right) scored three kills on 16 January 1944 with the 35th FS/8th FG to take his total to four. He claimed four more kills in P-38s during 1944 before returning to the US. He rejoined the 8th FG as group operations officer in 1945 (*John Stanaway*)

bombers were doing most of their operating at night, and the Jap fighter-bombers and fighters were trying our formations.

'On 16 January 1944 I was flying with a formation of 15 P-40Ns covering a landing at Saidor, New Guinea. Our four flights were stacked from 8000 ft up to 14,000 ft. Approximately 40 Jap fighters – "Tonys", "Hamps" and "Zekes" – came in from about 16,000 ft in neat four-ship formations. Our top and nearest flight called them in first, and turned into them. Our other flights started to gain altitude and turned into the Nips as they came down through us. The Japs made the mistake of losing their altitude advantage, and in the free-for-all that ensued they lost 19 aeroplanes. We had two holed. They kept their four-ship flights together, but their support seemed to go no further than that.'

The 19 victories scored by the 35th FS set a record for the highest total claimed by a single V Fighter Command squadron in one combat. Bill Gardner and 1Lt Lynn E Witt Jr tied for top honours with three confirmed victories each, while Bud Pool scored two kills. All three men would later become aces flying P-38s. Meanwhile, 1Lt Lee R Everhart's two victories brought his total to five, making him the 35th FS's second ace. He would score one further victory, flying a P-38, prior to being killed in action on 12 October 1944.

At the end of February 1944, the 35th FS turned in its Warhawks for new P-38Js. Its scores achieved while flying the P-40N support Davis's confidence in the Warhawk. From September 1943 to January 1944,

P-40N (possibly 42-105304) 'White 15' *Island Dream*, of the 7th FS/49th FG was the regular aircraft of Lt Roger Farrell. He scored three confirmed victories in late 1943 and early 1944 (*Dwayne Tabatt*)

the 35th FS was credited with 65 confirmed victories, while the two more experienced P-40 squadrons of the 49th FG scored a combined total of 67 kills during the same period. The 7th and 8th FSs continued to soldier on with their P-40Ns into the summer of 1944 before they too converted to the P-38. Although little aerial combat took place during this period, the 49th FG Warhawk pilots made the most of their opportunities.

On 23 January 1944, Jim Hagerstrom of the 8th FS was credited with four kills, bringing his total to six confirmed. Eight years later, while flying F-86 Sabres in Korea, he would become an ace all over again. Capt

These replacement pilots, seen here at Charters Towers, in Australia, in August 1943, would soon make their mark in the 49th FG, but only one would survive the war. Lt Don W Meuten (centre) became a six-victory ace with the 8th FS before dying in a flying accident in May 1944. Lt Philip E Kreichbaum (left) was killed in action on 2 November 1944 and Lt Jack A Fenimore flew P-40N 'White 28' *O'Riley's Daughter* with the 7th FS (*Steve Ferguson*)

P-40Ns of the 49th FG displayed some of the USAAF's best fighter nose art of the war. *Ragged But Right* was 'Yellow 65' of the 8th FS/49th FG, flown by 2Lt John Bodak. He destroyed two 'Hamps' with this aircraft on 23 January 1944, and added a third victory ten months later flying a P-38 (*Steve Ferguson*)

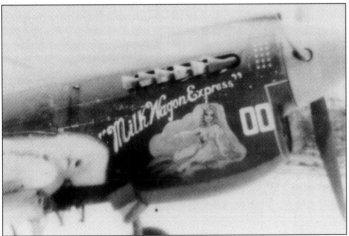

These two views are both of P-40N 'White 00' of the 7th FS/49th FG, and were taken at different times in 1944. Different names and nose art adorned either side of the cowling, while the propeller spinner was also modified in colour. It was standard practice for the pilot to choose the markings on the port side while the crew chief decorated the starboard *(Dwayne Tabatt)*

Arland Stanton of the 7th FS joined the ranks of the aces on 6 February, scoring the fifth of his eventual eight victories. And on 12 March 1Lt Donald W Meuten of the 8th FS claimed a triple kill over Wewak to become the last all-P-40 ace in the Pacific theatre. He was posted missing in action less than two months later. Then, on 7 May, 1Lt Bob DeHaven of the 7th FS scored his tenth victory, making him the second P-40 double ace in the theatre behind Capt Ernie Harris of the 8th FS.

THE LAST VICTORY

The 49th FG traded in its last P-40s in September 1944, marking the end of a long and successful run. But the Warhawk's combat career in the South Pacific was not yet over. The P-40Ns were refurbished and reassigned to other units. Some went to bomb groups for scouting, as well

This P-40N-15 of the 7th FS/49th FG was photographed at Biak in September 1944, shortly before the squadron replaced its Warhawks with P-38s. Its blue propeller spinner was a squadron identification marking (*Dwayne Tabatt*)

Sgt Ralph Winkle, a 71st TRG crew chief, poses with one of the hand-me-down P-40Ns which his unit obtained from the 49th FG when it converted to P-38s in the autumn of 1944. At this time, the Warhawk still carried the 8th FS markings of ace Bob White. Winkle later became crew chief for Medal of Honor winner (and 81st TRS CO) Capt William Shomo, who claimed seven kills on 11 January 1945 flying an F-6D Mustang (*Steve Ferguson*)

as local defence and general 'hack' duty, but the majority were assigned to the 71st Tactical Reconnaissance Group (TRG).

Between November 1944 and January 1945, the 110th TRS/71st TRG received credit for 14 enemy aircraft destroyed while flying P-40Ns during the invasion of the Philippines. On 29 January 1945, 2Lt Robert L Hammond of the 110th TRS was credited with the last known victory scored by a P-40 pilot in the Pacific theatre during World War 2. This is his combat report of that mission;

'I was flying wingman in a two-ship flight of P-40s attempting to find a hole in a solid overcast to continue a recon mission. We were flying south-east at 9000 ft, and at 0810 hrs over the Mamparing Mountains we observed a lone "Zeke" at three o'clock, travelling east at 10,000 ft. We immediately turned to the attack, following the Nip down in a shallow dive. We continued in a line-astern chase for four to five minutes. I was closing too fast, so I pulled up and to the left to slow my rate of closure. My flight leader then came in dead astern, opened fire at 500 yards and held it to 20 yards. Hits were observed in the wings and fuselage. My flight leader pulled up to the right and in front of the Nip.

'I then pulled down on the tail of the "Zeke" and gave him a burst, which went under his tail. I pulled up slightly and gave a second burst, and saw the left side of the Nip engine explode with a large orange flame. The "Zeke" then crashed, flaming into the ground and exploding. I followed him down to the ground and then returned to my formation and continued the mission.'

AT WAR IN THE ISLANDS

When Japanese forces occupied an obscure island at the eastern end of the Solomons chain in June 1942 and began building an airfield there, they set in motion a sequence of events which would soon capture worldwide attention. The existence of such a base on Guadalcanal would threaten the lightly-defended Allied positions in the New Hebrides and on New Caledonia, thus threatening the vital sea lanes carrying men and war materials from the United States to Australia.

Allied high command reacted decisively, and on 7 August 1942 US Marines invaded Guadalcanal. The Japanese did not oppose the landing, and within hours the unfinished airstrip was in American hands. But as construction crews rushed to complete the base, Japanese forces counter-attacked. The result was a bloody six-month campaign, but by the end of the year the Americans had gained the upper hand.

Initially, the only USAAF fighters involved in the Guadalcanal fighting were P-39 and P-400 Airacobras, but as the Army began to build its strength for the forthcoming push further up the Solomons chain, squadrons equipped with P-38 Lightnings and P-40 Warhawks joined the fight as units of the Thirteenth Air Force.

The Warhawks assigned to the Solomons were new P-40F models, which were equipped with licence-built versions of the Roll-Royce Merlin V-1650 engine instead of the Allison V-1710 used in previous models. The Merlin, which had gained fame as the powerplant of the RAF's Spitfire and Hurricane, featured a superior supercharging system that boosted the P-40's effective combat ceiling by several thousand feet. Reports coming back from the early air combats over Guadalcanal indicated that many encounters were taking place at altitudes of 20,000 ft and above, so it was felt that the P-40F would stand a better chance of success over the Solomons than the Allison-powered versions.

The Warhawk's baptism of fire at Guadalcanal came with the 68th FS/347th FG. The squadron had been flying patrols from Tongatubu, in the Tongan Islands, for six months before moving a detachment of P-40s up to Henderson Field, Guadalcanal, on 12 November 1942. The full squadron followed three weeks later, settling in at the newly-completed 'Fighter Two' strip with a mixed complement of P-39s and P-40s.

On 15 January 1943, while escorting B-17s assigned to attack five Japanese destroyers off Faisi, a flight of four P-40s from the 68th FS was attacked by enemy F1M 'Pete' float biplanes, and in the ensuing action nine Japanese aircraft were downed. Top scorer was Lt Lloyd G Huff with three confirmed victories. Further combats with the brave, but doomed, Japanese biplane pilots came on 18 and 20 January, netting five more kills.

A new P-40 unit, the 44th FS, together with P-38s and Marine F4Fs, joined the 68th FS in opposing an enemy raid against Guadalcanal on 27 January 1943. This was the first chance for the 44th FS to avenge the beating its P-40s had taken at Pearl Harbor more than a year earlier. Having spent the ensuing months in Hawaii before moving to New Caledonia in November 1942, the 44th was now the USAAF's only all-P-40 unit on Guadalcanal, having arrived on 20 January 1943 – just a week before its first action.

The Japanese tried a new tactic on 27 January when they sent about 30 Ki-43 'Oscar' fighters over Guadalcanal ahead of the bombers. Alerted by coast watchers posted further up the Solomons archipelago, P-38s and F4Fs took off to meet the attack. As battle was joined at 20,000 ft over the island, ten P-40Fs of the 44th and 68th FSs were also scrambled.

The Warhawks were just passing through 6000 ft when the lead flight was jumped by 'Oscars' diving out of the fight above. Two P-40s of the 68th FS were shot down and a third badly damaged before a flight of P-38s swooped down to break up the Ki-43s. A flight of four P-40Fs from the 44th FS, led by squadron commander Maj Kermit Tyler, then joined in. Tyler and his element leader, Pearl Harbor combat veteran Capt Ken Taylor, each claimed a probable kill, and their wingmen got one confirmed victory apiece. The wingmen, 1Lts Robert B Westbrook and Elmer M Wheadon, were both hit during the battle, but would go on to become aces in the 44th FS.

Thus began the outstanding combat history of the unit known as the 'Vampires'. Over the next 11 months it would establish itself as

When first assigned to Guadalcanal, the P-40Fs of the 44th FS carried only a single white band around their fuselages as a unit marking. 'White 106' *Irene* was assigned to Capt Sam Hitchcock, a flight leader. Note how the nose number repeats the last three digits of the aircraft's serial number (*Jim Sullivan*)

Capt Westbrook flew P-40M 'White 129' *Princess Pat II* during the summer of 1943. The aircraft displayed the nickname on both sides of the nose and seven Japanese flags below the windscreen. Note how the white stripes have worn away under the wings and across the top of the fuselage. Westbrook scored no victories in this aircraft (*Jack Cook*)

P-40Fs of the 44th (foreground) and 68th FSs display the 'starburst' white theatre marking stripes applied to Warhawks on Guadalcanal in early 1943. Capt Al Johnson flies 'White 102' (41-14825) *Miss Alma*, while 1Lt Ray Morrissey is in 41-14102. Ironically, both pilots were killed in action on the same day, 13 February 1943 (*Sam Hitchcock via Jack Cook*)

In some cases it takes a long time to become an ace. 1Lt Magnus W 'Maggie' Francis was officially credited with 4.5 confirmed victories when he completed his tour in the 44th FS in January 1944. In 1986 his credit for one Zero damaged on 1 July 1943 was upgraded to a confirmed victory, making him an ace. Francis died in a C-47 crash in 1948 (*Jack Cook*)

the highest scoring P-40 squadron of 1943, logging 117.5 confirmed victories before converting to P-38s at the end of the year.

The decision by the Japanese to withdraw their troops from Guadalcanal set the stage for several fierce aerial battles in February 1943. With Guadalcanal now in Allied hands, the Japanese were determined to keep hold of the northern Solomons, and they stepped up efforts to build new airfields on Bougainville and New Georgia. Allied commanders responded accordingly, sending B-24 Liberator and PB4Y heavy bombers to operate from Guadalcanal against the new targets. And on 21 February, Allied troops landed on three beaches in the Russell Islands, 30 miles west of Guadalcanal, for the express purpose of building a forward airfield.

The 44th FS was in action four times during February, scoring 11 confirmed victories. The biggest mission came on the 13th, when the squadron was assigned to escort B-24s on one of their first daylight strikes against enemy shipping in the Shortland-Buin area. The mission started badly, with three P-40s and two P-38s dropping out with mechanical problems. Once over the target, two of the six B-24s were shot down by ground fire, with a third badly damaged, and then 45 Japanese fighters pounced on the remaining B-24s and their six escorting fighters. The ensuing 50-minute battle ranged over 150 miles, and Capt Albert Johnson and Lt Raymond Morrissey of the 44th FS were shot down, although both were posthumously credited with confirmed victories during the fight. 1Lt Bob Westbrook scored his second victory, earning him a Silver Star, and another future ace, 2Lt Jack A Bade, scored a single kill, although his aircraft had been hit repeatedly. He was awarded the DSC.

Missions continued through the spring of 1943, but there was little contact made with enemy aircraft. During this time, the 18th FG moved its headquarters to Guadalcanal, the unit being comprised of the 44th FS, together with two P-39 squadrons. It was also during this period that a complex design of recognition stripes was added to the fuselage, wings and tail of 44th and 68th FS Warhawks. The 68th went one step further, adorning its P-40Fs with large sharkmouths on their noses. In mid-year the Thirteenth Air Force adopted a marking scheme for its P-40s which included an all-white tail.

The summer of 1943 would bring success to the 44th FS as the 'Vampire' pilots ran up impressive scores during three months of heavy combat. Meanwhile, the 68th FS exchanged its P-40s for P-39s, while the 70th FS/18th FS supplemented its Airacobras with P-40s. The Royal New Zealand Air Force's No 14 Sqn, equipped with Lend-Lease P-40K and P-40M Kittyhawks, also joined the fight at this time, while the 44th FS started receiving the P-40M (a reduced-weight version of the Allison-powered Warhawk) to replace its well-worn P-40Fs.

1Lt Jack Bade's well worn P-40F 'White 111' was named *Destitute Prostitute* on the port side and *Reckless Prostitute* on the starboard side (*Jack Cook*)

1Lt Jack A Bade scored five victories and one probable in the 44th FS on Guadalcanal between 4 February and 30 June 1943. After the war he became a test pilot for Republic Aviation and was killed in the crash of an F-105 in 1963 (*Grant Smith via Jack Cook*)

Capt Westbrook's groundcrew pose with their P-40F, 'White 104', after Westbrook scored his fifth victory on 12 June 1943. They are, from left to right, John Gorman, crew chief Hank Straub and George Dixer (*Jack Cook*)

On 5 June the quiet period ended for the 44th FS. During an escort mission to Buin Harbor, at Kahili, the squadron ran into a mixed force of Japanese interceptors, including Zeros and 'Rufe' and 'Dave' floatplanes. 1Lt Robert C Byrnes and 2Lt Magnus W 'Maggie' Francis (both future aces) each shot down a Zero, but one P-40 was lost and Jack Bade was wounded when he took on ten Zeros which were attacking several Marine bombers despite his guns being jammed.

Exactly one week later the 44th FS was able to acclaim its first aces, and not surprisingly one of them was Bob Westbrook. On that morning P-40s of the 44th were part of a force of 91 US and New Zealand fighters which were scrambled to intercept 50 Zeros over the Russell Islands. Westbrook and his wingman, Lt Bob Byrnes, were among the first to make contact. Westbrook fired a long burst into a Zero and saw it fall into the sea to claim his fifth victory. Byrnes, meanwhile, picked off a second Zero which was attempting to get on Westbrook's tail.

The squadron's other new ace was New Yorker 1Lt Henry E Matson. One of the many pilots from Flying Class 42-G who joined the 44th straight from flight school in the summer of 1942, his victory on 12 June brought his final total to five. Matson's most memorable combat had

taken place five days earlier when, on 7 June, he claimed two victories, the second of which he crashed into head-on. Although burned and scratched, Matson was able to bale out of his P-40 and avoid the attention of three Zeros which seemed poised to strafe him in his parachute. He landed in the water, pulled himself into his dinghy and was rescued by a crash boat two hours later. Matson returned to the US in August 1943 and spent the rest of the war as a P-47 instructor.

The 44th's biggest scoring day of the war came on 16 June when its pilots were credited with 19 confirmed victories. This action came about when the Japanese sent 50 'Val' dive-bombers, escorted by 30 Zeros, to

By the summer of 1943 the tail surfaces of Warhawks in the Solomon Islands were painted solid white to further distinguish them from inline-engined Ki-61 'Tonys' of the JAAF. Shown here at 'Fighter Two' airstrip on Guadalcanal, 'White 116' was the regular aircraft of 44th FS ace 1Lt Henry E Matson (five victories) and 'White 111' was flown by ace 1Lt Jack Bade (*Frank Crain via Jack Cook*)

1Lt Henry E Matson was one of the many graduates of Flying Class 42-G who became aces in the 44th FS, scoring five confirmed victories and one probable. His best day in combat was 2 June 1943, when he brought down two 'Zekes' of the 251st AG, including one flown by ace PO Masuaki Endo, who rammed Matson head-on. The American parachuted safely – Endo did not (*Henry Matson via Jack Cook*)

63

Capt Robert C Byrnes completed 115 combat missions with the 44th FS during 1943, scoring five victories and a probable. He achieved his first four kills during a hectic 11-day period in June 1943, and completed his scoring with one 'Val' destroyed and another probable on 31 August 1943 (*Robert Holman via Jack Cook*)

A boyish-looking 1Lt Cyrus Gladen climbs into the cockpit of his P-40F 'White 115' *Fugari* at Segi airstrip, Munda, in October 1943. Gladen, another Class 42-G graduate, scored in groups – he was credited with two 'Zekes' destroyed on 16 June 1943 and three 'Vals' on the last day of August (*Jack Cook*)

1Lt Joseph J Lesicka of the 44th FS scored five victories in a single mission on 15 July 1943 flying his P-40M 'White 125' *Gypsy Rose Lee*. The top-scoring Warhawk ace of the squadron with nine confirmed victories at the end of his first tour, Lesicka returned to the 44th FS as CO in 1944, and later moved to 18th FG headquarters (*Frank Crain via Jack Cook*)

attack American cargo ships off Guadalcanal. More than 100 Allied fighters scrambled to oppose them, and four flights of 44th FS P-40s were patrolling at about 23,000 ft above the ships when about 30 of the escorted 'Vals' were spotted. For once, the Warhawk pilots had an altitude advantage and they made the most of it. One of the 44th pilots involved was 2Lt Cyrus R 'Cy' Gladen, who was flying as wingman to Bob Byrnes. He later gave this account of the action;

'As I pushed the stick forward, I saw that a Zero had rolled out of his left turn, and I immediately hopped on him, giving him a long burst. He started to smoke and go down in a left-hand diving turn. This "clinched the meat" for my P-40, and I poured another long burst into him. He started burning and I pulled out. The Zero went down between Savo and Lunga Point.

'I pulled up into a turn and another Zero was off to my right. I got in a good shot and undoubtedly it hit him – he was going much faster than I was, and he rolled out and flew straight away from me. By this time he was about 400 yards away. Most of my guns had stopped firing, and I shot at him with my two remaining guns. My tracers seemed to be hitting him. He was smoking and I continued firing. I exhausted my ammunition and continued on the Zero's tail until I began gaining speed on him. I saw his left wing was burning and puffs of white smoke were coming out. His right wing was badly shot up.

'I flew up beside the aeroplane and saw the pilot. I couldn't tell if he was alive or not, but he seemed to be slumped over. He was going down rapidly and he passed into a cloud. I turned back and landed to get more ammunition, but by that time there was no longer a flight close by.'

A smiling Capt Frank L Gaunt of the 44th FS poses in the cockpit of his P-40M after scoring three victories on 15 July 1943. Gaunt recorded his seventh, and last, P-40 kill a month later, and completed his scoring with a P-38 victory on 11 November 1943. He flew a second tour in P-51s with the 325th FG in Italy, then became a physician after the war (*Jack Cook*)

Gladen, a Minnesota boy and pre-war aircraft mechanic, had scored his first two victories. He would achieve a triple kill on 31 August 1943 to earn a place on the list of 44th FS aces, and by January 1944, when he returned to the US, Cy Gladen had flown 164 combat missions and was the holder of a DFC and 20 Air Medals. Other future aces scoring their first victories on 16 June were 1Lts L B 'Bob' Shuler, Frank L Gaunt, Coatsworth B Head Jr and Joseph J Lesicka. Head was the top scorer among them, with two Zeros and a 'Val' confirmed destroyed. In all, the Allied defenders claimed 97 victories during the one-hour battle.

ON THE OFFENSIVE

On 30 June 1943 the Allies invaded Rendova Island and New Georgia (the latter was the site of the strategic airfield at Munda), triggering a new round of aerial battles over the Solomon chain. From then until Munda was captured on 5 August, the 44th FS scored no fewer than 50.5 victories, creating seven more aces. On the second day of the campaign the squadron was again highly successful in its defence of the invasion fleet between Rendova Harbor and Munda Point. Again, the Japanese sent 'Vals' with heavy escort to attack the ships, and again the Warhawk pilots extracted a heavy toll. One of them, 1Lt Mel Wheadon, became an ace in a day when he was credited with five victories. This is his combat report;

'On a patrol to Rendova, covering shipping at 5000 ft, I heard Westbrook call "Tally-Ho", and at the same instant saw a flight of enemy dive-bombers at "twelve o'clock" from me, peeling off for a run at our shipping. My flight moved right in on them, and we shot down seven dive-bombers – I got four. This action took place low over the water, and didn't last long. All of a sudden there just didn't seem to be anything to shoot at, so I started forming my flight.

The 44th FS scoreboard serves as a backdrop for four pilots following an awards ceremony in the summer of 1943. They are, from left to right, 1Lt Douglas V Currey (three victories), Capt Elmer M 'Doc' Wheadon (seven victories), 1Lt Charles T Sackett (missing on 14 September 1943) and Capt Jack A Bade (five victories) (*Jack Cook*)

1Lt Doc Wheadon points to his first victory flag on the 44th FS scoreboard in front of the operations shack at 'Fighter Two' on Guadalcanal in June 1943. Shortly afterwards, on 1 July, Wheadon destroyed four 'Vals' and a 'Zeke' in a single combat to become the first P-40 'ace-in-a-day' of the Solomon Islands campaign (*Jack Cook*)

Westbrook called me and said there was a hell of a fight south-west of where he was, and to come on up. We headed for them, but the action wasn't very good. I did get on the tail of a Zero and gave him the works. Fired at another and ran out of ammunition. My fun was over then and there. I had to get the hell out as I was without any guns to help me.

'Things went well for me until some joker got on my tail. He started firing out of range, which was a good warning for me. Being at 2000 ft, there was only one direction to go, and that was toward a beautiful rain squall that I saw three F4Fs and a P-40 go into. So I headed for it. The only evasive action I made was to rotate the stick around the cockpit with both hands and kick rudders as hard as I could first one way and then another. My aeroplane partially stalled and fell off on a wing, which made me turn slightly to cover. When I looked back at my pursuer, he was

Even aces have bad days in the cockpit. 2Lt Cotesworth B Head Jr poses with a P-40F of the 44th FS which he wrecked at Efate in November 1942 while the squadron was in the final stages of training. Head redeemed his reputation, scoring eight victories in P-40s and six more in P-38s before being lost on 18 January 1944 (*Jack Cook*)

Capt Frank Gaunt peels off in his P-40M 'White 126' *The Twerp* as fellow ace Lt Cy Gladen prepares to follow in Lt Frank Crain's 'White 134'. This shot shows the 44th FS markings system in the summer of 1943 to good effect. Later, white bars were added to the national insignias for increased visibility (*Jack Cook*)

1Lt L B 'Bob' Shuler of the 68th FS poses his P-40F-15 41-19831 'White 208' for a nice flying shot in the spring of 1943 before his transfer to the 44th FS. Pilots and aircraft of the 44th, 68th and 70th FSs on Guadalcanal often intermingled on missions during this period before the Warhawks were concentrated in the 44th FS (*Jack Cook*)

pulling away. He had either thought I was going down or got discouraged as hell from the contortions my aeroplane was going through. My flight accounted for nine aeroplanes on this day.'

Another pilot in the fight was 1Lt Magnus W Francis. A member of the 42-G class, Francis became an ace on 1 July without ever knowing it. After the mission he was credited with 3.5 victories and one damaged to add to a single kill scored on 5 June. He went home in 1944 with an official score of 4.5 confirmed victories and failed to score again during a second combat tour in Burma with the 1st Air Commando Group in 1945. Magnus was killed in a C-47 crash in 1948. In 1986 the US Air Force upgraded his 1 July 1943 damaged claim to give him a total of 5.5 victories.

On 15 July, following the next big fight over Munda, the 44th FS was able to boast two more aces after 1Lt Frank Gaunt shot down three Zeros

1Lt Bob Shuler scored his seventh, and last, victory on 10 August 1943 while flying one of several P-40Rs assigned to the 44th FS. This rare Warhawk version was a long-tail P-40F or P-40L powered by an Allison V-1710-81 engine in place of its original Merlin powerplant. Only 300 were built (*Mrs L B Shuler*)

to bring his total to six confirmed and 1Lt Joe Lesicka achieved five kills to become the squadron's top scorer with eight confirmed. Lesicka would add one more before the end of his tour. Then, on 4 August, Lts C B Head and Bob Shuler joined the roster of aces. Shuler gave this account of his actions during a fight with 25 Zeros over Rendova;

'I picked out one that had passed under us in a dive. I thought at first that he might be a dive-bomber, but later saw that he was a Zero. Firing a few bursts in the dive, I really got him as he pulled out. I saw him hit the beach and explode. Using my speed, I increased my altitude and got back into the fight. I levelled off and found another Zero in my sights. A long burst from my guns caused him to flame and explode in mid-air.

'Turning to the left, I found myself in a similar position as before – another Zero approached at close range. I opened fire and saw my tracers converging on the Nip. His wings began to rock and he fell off into a vertical roll. I followed him down, firing all the way along. The aeroplane started blazing from the cockpit, came out of the roll and went into a slight dive. The canopy came off and the pilot stood up with one leg on the wing and the other inside the aeroplane. Pulling the parachute ripcord before he left the cockpit, both the aeroplane and the parachute went down in flames.

'As I turned off onto the fourth Zero that passed about 500 ft above me, I closed in and opened fire. Although I seemed to have been getting hits, the Zero didn't want to burn, but I continued firing until his left wing and cockpit flamed. I tagged onto another Zero, but my guns were out of ammunition after the first burst.'

With the airfield at Munda in friendly hands from 5 August, the Allies now had an air base 170 miles closer to Japanese bases in the northern Solomons. Vella Lavella fell in mid-September, setting the stage for the invasion of Bougainville, the capture of which would neutralise the Japanese stronghold at Rabaul. The 44th FS scored its final P-40 victories

Crew chief S/Sgt Jim Cooley sits in the cockpit of P-40F 'White 111' in the late summer of 1943. The significance of the 14 victory flags on the starboard side scoreboard is unclear, but they may indicate the number of kills scored by P-40s looked after by Cooley (*Jim Cooley via Jack Cook*)

and acknowledged its last two P-40 aces – Bob Byrnes and Cy Gladen – during this period.

Bob Westbrook was promoted to major and became CO of the 44th FS on 25 September. About two weeks later, on 10 October 1943, he scored the squadron's first victory in a P-38 while on a mission with the 339th FS. The Warhawk era in the Solomon Islands was now rapidly coming to a close – the last three P-40 kills by the 44th FS were recorded on 8 November 1943, and soon afterwards the squadron converted to P-38s.

Westbrook went on to become the Thirteenth Air Force's top ace with 13 P-38 victories in addition to his seven P-40 kills. Similarly, Capt C B Head continued scoring after the 44th FS converted to P-38s. Neither man would survive the war, however, Head being killed in action on 18 January 1944 after scoring his 14th victory and Westbrook going down ten months later while strafing a freighter in the Makassar Strait.

TAN WARHAWKS

The pilots of the 45th FS/15th FG at Bellows Field, Hawaii, were ecstatic when, during summer 1943, they were told by their commanding officer, Maj Julian 'Jack' Thomas, that they were being ordered into combat. For more than 18 months after the Pearl Harbor attack, the 15th FG had been stuck in what had become a backwater, flying endless patrols over Oahu, and scrambling occasionally to intercept suspicious aircraft which always turned out to be friendly ones that had strayed off course.

In September 1943 the 45th FS moved to lonely Baker Island, a tiny coral outcrop in the Ellice Island group that is virtually devoid of vegetation, and some 1650 miles south-west of Hawaii. It was equipped with new P-40Ns, camouflaged in a pinkish tan over light blue to blend in with the surroundings.

Seventh Air Force had established a fighter base at Baker in preparation for assaults against the Japanese-held Gilbert Islands, about 600 miles to the west. But the pilots were soon disappointed to realise that their most dangerous foes were the swarms of house flies that infested the island.

The top ace of the Thirteenth Air Force with 20 victories, Lt Col Robert B 'Westy' Westbrook started by flying P-40s in the 44th FS. He was promoted to command the squadron in September 1943, by which time he had scored seven victories in Warhawks. Westbrook was shot down and killed in a P-38 while strafing a Japanese ship on 22 November 1944 (*Jack Cook*)

Maj Julian E 'Jack' Thomas commanded the 45th FS/15th FG during the Marshall Islands campaign. Known as an innovator and a strong supporter of the P-40, Thomas named his aircraft after his wife, whose nickname was Jickie. He was killed in action on 15 June 1945 in a P-51 while leading the 15th FG on a mission over Japan (*Jack Lambert*)

JICKIE VI (the P-40N-5 assigned to Maj Jack Thomas) has an experimental rocket launcher mounted outboard of the bomb racks. The rockets proved a failure. Note also the plywood sway braces fitted to the bomb racks. The 45th FS P-40Ns were painted tan over light blue to blend into the surroundings on the coral islands where they were based (*Jack Lambert*)

An epidemic of bacillary dysentery hit the squadron in October, eventually infecting 91 men, and forcing Thomas to suspend flying for four days while they recovered.

The only break in the tedium came on 23 October when radar picked up a track passing south of the island at 12,000 ft. A pair of P-40Ns from the 45th FS was scrambled and flight leader Capt Gilmer 'Buck' Snipes radioed a 'Tally-Ho' call 22 minutes later. The bogey was a four-engined Japanese 'Emily' flying boat, which Snipes promptly shot down to record the squadron's first confirmed victory.

The 45th moved up to Nanoumea Island after the bloody invasion of Tarawa in late November, where it was soon reinforced by the arrival of 13 training-weary P-40Ks from by the escort carrier USS *Breton*. Action still eluded the 45th even after a move in December to Abamama Island, a pleasant spot in the southern Gilberts. Thomas led a detachment of eight P-40Ns to Makin Island on 17 January 1944 so that the Warhawks were at last within striking distance of the enemy. The 45th FS began

Lt George H Dunlap takes off from the USS *Breton* in P-40K 'White 203' (42-46178), this aircraft having been reassigned from the 8th FS to replace war-weary 45th FS P-40Ns in the Marshalls campaign in December 1943. The pilots of the 45th FS considered their 'new' aircraft worse than the ones they replaced (*Jim Sullivan*)

operations the following day with a mission against the Japanese stronghold at Jaluit Atoll, some 300 miles to the north-east. The P-40Ns pounded Jaluit and Mili with bombs, gunfire and even experimental rockets throughout January. Enemy ground fire could be intense on these missions, but the Japanese put up no aerial opposition.

At the same time B-25s of the 41st BG at Makin were taking a beating from Japanese fighters when they ventured farther north to Maloelap Atoll, beyond the range of P-39s and P-40s of VII Fighter Command. On these missions intercepting Zeros would chase the withdrawing B-25s as far south as Arno Atoll, and Lt Col Sherwood Buckland, director of VII Fighter Command at Makin, saw an opportunity to give the B-25 crews some relief by arranging a trap for the Zeros. Rather than escorting the B-25s outbound as far as Arno, the 45th FS would meet them on the way back and perhaps get a shot at the pursuing Zeros in the process. Careful planning was needed, together with expert airmanship by the 12 P-40 pilots who had to stretch their fuel to maximum range, and still make a precise rendezvous with the bombers. Led by Maj Harry M Thompson, the 45th FS did just that.

With three flights stepped up at 8000, 10,000 and 12,500 ft, they passed Arno and kept going north. Just as their belly tanks were running dry, the P-40 pilots spotted the B-25s on the deck over Aur Atoll with about 15 Zeros of the 252nd Naval Air Group harassing them. Capt James Vande Hey, leading the middle flight, was first to attack, and he quickly shot at two A6Ms which blew up. Soon all 12 P-40s were engaged, including 1Lt D R 'Bob' Butler. He recalled;

'I looked out to my right and a "Zeke" pulled up from below in a steep climb. I had eye contact with the pilot and he pulled away. I was surprised at the quickness of his climb – much better than the P-40 could do. I continued toward Maloelap and turned around, making contact with another "Zeke" heading home and was able to get a victory. I remember that none of the Japanese aeroplanes had mutual support, to my surprise. They were always on their own. My kill was recorded on the (gun camera) film, and I was told it was used in many classes back home I never did see the film.'

TWEEDIE II was the P-40N-5 (42-105109) assigned to 1Lt Dwight R 'Bob' Butler in the 45th FS/15th FG. Seen here at Abemama Atoll in 1944, it is loaded with a drop tank and two 500-lb bombs for a mission to Mili. Butler, who scored one victory in the squadron's big fight on 26 January 1944, named *TWEEDIE II* after his future wife (*George Hunter*)

1Lt Arthur H Bridge and his crew chief examine *Miss Cappy*, the P-40N-5 assigned to them with the 45th FS, at Makin in March 1944. Twenty-four mission markers in the shape of bombs adorn the fuselage. Note how the aircraft has been repainted in sand over light blue, although the wheel centres remain neutral grey (*George Dunlap*)

Another 45th FS pilot to claim a victory was 1Lt Robert W 'Todd' Moore, a long-serving member of the 15th FG who was leading the high flight. He reported;

'After all the aeroplanes had passed beneath me, I dropped down to pick up stragglers. Between 6000 and 7000 ft I spotted a Zero that was attempting to flee from the fight. The pilot saw me just about the time I saw him and we turned into each other. Apparently, he decided to change his tactics then – he went into a shallow high-speed dive directly toward Taroa Airfield. I continued my front-quarter run on him and, as he continued his dive, I scored multiple hits in his engine and wing root area.

'I knew better than to try to dogfight with a "Zeke" in a P-40, but I did manage a tight turn onto this "Zeke's" tail. The pilot tried two or three violent skids to throw off my aim and then the "Zeke" did a very strange thing. It slowly turned over onto its back. It seemed as if the pilot was seriously injured. I closed to about 700 ft from him and opened fire with a lead slightly below the descending fighter. The "Zeke" exploded in my face. After the fight was over, I felt relief amounting to exhilaration.'

All 12 P-40s returned safely from the mission, their pilots claiming ten victories and two probables. The squadron tried to repeat its success on further missions during the next two days but failed to contact enemy fighters. Then the P-40s returned to pound Jaluit and Mili in preparation for the invasion of the Marshall Islands. But never again did the P-40Ns of the 45th FS encounter Japanese aircraft, for with the end of the aerial campaign in the Marshalls the unit returned to Hawaii in March 1944.

The central Pacific deployment had suited the 45th's pilots well, for a year later, equipped with P-51D Mustangs, many returned to action at Iwo Jima, flying very long range escort missions to Japan until the end of the war. During these missions, Todd Moore was credited with downing 11 more aircraft to become the top ace of the Seventh Air Force during World War 2.

Capt Gordon Hyde sits in the cockpit of Lt R H 'Todd' Moore's P-40N-5. The aircraft displays Moore's full record for the central Pacific campaign – 17 missions and one aerial victory scored on the 45th's single big P-40 action on 26 January 1944. Moore later became top ace of the Seventh Air Force with 12 victories (*Jack Lambert*)

THE FORGOTTEN FRONT

The Aleutian Islands are actually the peaks of a volcanic mountain range that stretches across the Northern Pacific Ocean from the tip of the Alaskan Peninsula some 1100 miles toward the Asian Continent. These barren, sparsely inhabited islands were virtually unknown outside Alaska before World War 2. Their strategic value, though, was clearly understood by the Alaska Defence Command and its colourful commander, Maj Gen Simon Bolivar Buckner.

As Buckner pressed his small command during 1941 to prepare for war with Japan, he knew his country would ignore the Aleutian chain at its peril. Left unguarded, the islands could provide Japan with naval and air bases from which to dominate the North Pacific. Worse, they could become a staging area for an assault on North America. Gaining a foothold in Alaska would place Japanese forces only hours away by air from the United States mainland. On the other hand, if the US could hold the Aleutians, the islands might serve similar purposes in the fight against Japan. As so often happens in wartime, the events that unfolded would yield a little of both.

The Aleutian Islands may have had great strategic value, but it would be hard to find a more difficult location on earth in which to conduct military operations. Forming a barrier between the North Pacific and the Bering Sea, the 279 islands are battered by storms, bare of vegetation and occasionally blanketed by smoke and ash from erupting volcanos. Their mountain peaks rise 6000 ft and more out of the sea, creating serious hazards for aviators. Similarly, the cold seas that surround the islands are notoriously rough, making naval operations uncomfortable at best. But it is the perpetual bad weather that leaves the greatest impression on those who venture to the Aleutians.

Day after day, week after week, the sky is stone grey, just like the land. Then a storm will blow in, with winds rising to 100 mph. The wind was known to actually flip parked aircraft on to their backs and roll up sections of the steel Marsten mats which served as paving on runways and dispersal areas. Most notorious is the 'williwaw', a high wind which can blow up in the course of a few minutes, turning a barely passable flying day into a horror show.

Just as lethal is the fog which forms quickly and is perhaps the Aleutians' least appealing feature. It was not unusual for a pilot to taxi out of his revetment under bright sunshine, only to find his airfield completely fogged in by the time he turned onto the runway for take-off. Obviously, that was preferable to looking down from the cockpit as a fog bank rolled in and blotted out the airfield when he was about to land. Nothing good awaited the pilot caught aloft by the fog. Although they are located on roughly the same latitude as the British Isles, the Aleutians can experience snowfall in any month of the year. Then, if the sun comes out, its warmth turns even the least travelled roads and paths through the volcanic soil of the islands into a thick, black goo.

Unsuited though the Aleutians were for a military campaign, war would come to the islands within a few months of America's entry into conflict. When the Japanese attacked Pearl Harbor on 7 December 1941, there was just one American fighter squadron stationed in Alaska. The 18th PS, equipped with P-36s, had arrived at Anchorage in February 1941, toward the beginning of the Alaska build-up. The only other combat units there were two bomb squadrons, equipped with obsolete B-18s.

If the aerial forces were meagre, the facilities were even worse. Although Buckner's command had been working furiously to build new military airfields, only two major bases – Elmendorf Field in Anchorage and Ladd Field in Fairbanks, plus several auxiliary fields – were operational in Alaska when the US entered the war. The only American military installation in the Aleutians was a Navy facility at the fishing port of Dutch Harbor on Unalaska Island at the eastern end of the chain.

Expecting the Japanese to strike Alaska soon after Pearl Harbor, Buckner's command redoubled its construction efforts. The Aleutians had top priority and work soon began on airfields at Cold Bay, on the southern tip of the Alaska Peninsula, and at Otter Point on Umnak Island, some 60 miles from Dutch Harbor, and the nearest suitable site for an airfield.

Meanwhile, a second Army pursuit squadron, the 11th, arrived at the end of December 1941 equipped with P-40Es. On 5 February, the Army's Alaska air units were unified as the Eleventh Air Force, and a few weeks later the 18th PS exchanged its worn-out P-36s for new P-40Es. As winter turned to spring, more USAAF units were on their way to Alaska, including four squadrons of P-39 Airacobras and one equipped with P-38E Lightnings. Small numbers of B-17s, B-24s and new B-26 Marauders bolstered the Eleventh's bomber strength.

———— ACTION AT DUTCH HARBOR ————

On 20 May 1942, Japanese warships of the 2nd Carrier Striking Force steamed out of their anchorage in the Inland Sea and headed north toward the Aleutian Islands. Formed around the light carriers *Junyo* and *Ryujo*, the force had orders to attack the American base at Dutch Harbor in a diversionary raid the day before a planned major confrontation with the US Navy at Midway Island. Having broken the Japanese radio code American naval intelligence soon became aware of this plan. Anchorage was informed, and on 22 May the 11th FS was ordered to move from Elmendorf Field to the new airfields at Cold Bay and Umnak. Most of the pilots and aircraft went to Umnak, while the ground echelon settled at Cold Bay, followed shortly by P-40Es of the 18th FS.

By 1 June 17 P-40Es and six B-26s were on alert at Umnak, expecting a Japanese attack at any moment. Capt Milton Ashkins was in command of the 11th FS detachment, pending arrival of the squadron CO, Capt John S Chennault. Conditions were miserable in the early days. A single 5000-ft runway, just 100 ft wide, had been scraped out of the tundra at Otter Point and paved with pierced-steel-planking Marsten mats, the first such application in a combat zone. Dispersal areas and revetments were not yet constructed so aircraft had to be parked along the side of the

Capt John S Chennault was 11th FS CO at the time of the Dutch Harbor attacks on 3-4 June 1942 and assumed command of the 343rd FG several months later. The son of legendary American Volunteer Group and Fourteenth Air Force commander Claire Chennault, he scored the 11th's FS last confirmed victory of the war when he shot down a Zero floatplane over Kiska on 25 September 1942 (*Joe Conner*)

1Lt Jacob W Dixon, shown here with a P-40E of the 11th FS, shared credit with 1Lt John B Murphy for shooting down a Japanese reconnaissance aircraft on 3 June 1942 over Umnak Pass – the first hostile aircraft destroyed by the Eleventh Air Force in World War 2. Murphy went on to become an ace in the European theatre, flying P-51s with the 359th FG (*Jake Dixon*)

runway. There were no permanent buildings, with the result that pilots and ground personnel were quartered in tents staked out on the soggy ground.

The communication links from Dutch Harbor to the fighter bases failed when the first Japanese raid occurred on the morning of 3 June. While a force of 'Kate' bombers and Zero fighters pounded installations at Dutch Harbor, P-40s of the 11th remained peacefully on the ground at Otter Point, just 70 miles away. Later that day, after reports of the raid reached Umnak, the 11th FS launched standing patrols to guard against a possible follow-up attack. The Japanese fleet did launch a second raid, but bad weather forced it to abort. However, four E8N 'Dave' floatplanes were sent to search for a reported US destroyer force, and two had the misfortune to be spotted over Umnak Pass, near Otter Point, by pilots 1Lt John B Murphy and 2Lt Jacob W Dixon. The 11th FS history describes what happened next;

'All of our aeroplanes were in the air and had been in formation out on patrol. 1Lt Murphy was the first one to spot two Japanese naval scout aeroplanes. He pulled away from the formation and evidently thought the others would follow him. His wingman was Lt Dixon. Murphy fired just two shots at the aeroplanes. One of the aeroplanes was hit, and it crashed into the bay at the end of the runway. The other disappeared into the clouds and got away.'

Jake Dixon recalled the event 60 years later in a telephone interview;

'It happened so quick you wouldn't believe it. There was a moment when I didn't know whether to shoot or not. Then I put a good load into him, and he went down near Ship Rock.'

Murphy and Dixon were each given credit for the downed aircraft, the first USAAF aerial victory of the Aleutian campaign. Dixon said he didn't see Murphy's attack, and believes they may have shot at different aircraft, but he never pressed the claim. He continued flying in the Aleutians until late in 1942 when a bout of pneumonia sent him home. Dixon served as a gunnery instructor for the rest of the war, but returned to combat during the Korean conflict and eventually retired from the USAF with the rank of colonel. Murphy, meanwhile, returned to the US in January 1943 and was assigned to the 359th FG, then in training. He resumed combat with the 359th in England, scoring a further 6.25 victories during 1944 flying P-47s and P-51s.

The Japanese task force launched another raid against Dutch Harbor during the afternoon of 4 June. Again they were able to bomb and strafe the port installations without interference from the 11th FS, but this time the Warhawk pilots caught up with them on the way home. A B-17 had just taken off from Otter Point when it radioed that it was under attack by enemy aircraft. A flight of four P-40s patrolling nearby heard the alarm and dived to attack, while four more P-40s scrambled from Otter Point.

The 18th FS tail markings are clearly visible on P-40E 40-389, seen here at Attu in 1944. Originally assigned to the 11th FS, 40-389 was the aircraft flown by 2Lt Herbert C White when he shot down a 'Val' dive-bomber over Umnak Pass on 4 June 1942 (*Morris Boynton*)

T/Sgt Joe Conner, 11th FS crew chief, poses proudly in front of the 'Aleutian Tiger' nose art applied to 11th FS P-40s after the Dutch Harbor engagements. The decoration honoured squadron commander Jack Chennault and his father, who commanded the 'Flying Tigers'. The shrouds around the exhaust pipes on this P-40E were part of the cold weather gear installed on the aircraft (*Joe Connor*)

A short but fierce combat took place practically over the airfield while the B-17 escaped. The P-40s immediately shot down two 'Vals', and at least one more crashed while attempting to return to its carrier. These kills were credited to 2Lts Lester M Chancellor, James A Dale and Herbert C White Jr. In addition, 2Lt John J Cape Jr destroyed a Zero, but was shot down himself. His P-40 was seen to dive straight into Umnak Pass, just off Otter Point, but no trace of Cape or his aircraft were ever found. The air base at Otter Point was later renamed in honour of the popular 23-year-old pilot from Cambridge, Massachusetts. A second P-40, flown by 2Lt Winfield E McIntyre, also was shot down, but McIntyre survived the subsequent crash landing.

Capt John S Chennault, son of the legendary commander of the American Volunteer Group in China, Claire L Chennault, arrived at Umnak on 5 June to find the 11th FS in a state of high excitement. The squadron gave itself the nickname 'Aleutian Tigers' in honour of Chennault's father, and soon afterward the men painted large Bengal tiger faces on the cowlings of their P-40s. But there would be no more air battles over

Umnak. The Japanese fleet pulled back, leaving occupation troops on the islands of Kiska and Attu further down the chain. A new phase of the Aleutian air war soon began.

THE 'KISKA BLITZ'

The 11th and the 18th FSs remained on high alert throughout the summer of 1942 but saw no further action, although the discovery of Japanese troops on Kiska and Attu sparked an immediate response from the Eleventh Air Force. Long-range B-24s and B-17s flew their first mission against Kiska on 11 June. But their target was more than 700 miles from Umnak, far beyond the range of the P-40s. Both fighter units would have to wait until a new base was opened on Adak, some 275 miles from Kiska, that September before they could return to the fight.

P-38s of the 54th FS took up station at Adak on 12 September, and detachments of P-40s from the 11th and 18th FSs arrived soon afterwards. Completing the force at Adak was a squadron of P-39s, plus No 14 Sqn Royal Canadian Air Force (RCAF), equipped with Kittyhawks.

The first maximum effort raid against Kiska by Eleventh Air Force aircraft at Adak came on 14 September 1942 but no P-40s took part. Then on 25 September 18 P-40s and 14 P-39s accompanied two B-17s and seven B-24s on a mission to strafe and bomb Kiska Harbor. This is the 11th FS intelligence report of the mission;

'The P-40s, led by Lt Col Chennault, and the P-39s, led by Maj (Wilbur) Miller, followed the routes shown on the map. The P-40s went in a short time before the P-39s. Lt (Albert) Aiken and his wingman, who were acting as top cover for the pursuit, encountered two float Zeros, one of which shot a 20 mm shell into the tail and a 0.30-cal shell into the wing tank of Lt Aiken's aeroplane. The Zero was shot down by Sqn Ldr (Kenneth) Boomer, and the pilot jumped into the harbour from a height of 50 ft. The squadron continued their strafing mission and hit gun emplacements, the camp area and a radar. They then swung around North Head and encountered another Zero, which, Lt Col Chennault reports, tried to ram him head-on after he was shot. They then turned left

Kittyhawk 'A' of No 14 Sqn RCAF receives attention at Cape Field, Umnak, in April 1943. RCAF Kittyhawk pilots participated in 60 missions during the 'Kiska Blitz' (*John Cloe*)

Mechanics change the engine of a 344th FS P-40K in the open at Shemya. Groundcrews in the Aleutians overcame horrendous conditions to keep an ageing fleet of Warhawks operational during 1944-45 (*Doyle Hicks*)

Groundcrews in the Aleutians faced challenges unlike those in any other combat zone. The crew chief of this 11th FS P-40K pulled back the canopy one winter morning at Cold Bay to find that high winds had blown snow through the seals, filling the cockpit (*Jake Dixon*)

and attacked an enemy submarine, which broke water outside the harbour. They killed the personnel operating the guns and believe that they damaged the submarine with their armour-piercing 0.50s. It was forced to submerge.

'Maj (Edgar) Romberg led four P-40s acting as protection for the bombers. He reports no sign of enemy aircraft at that altitude. After the bombers had completed their mission and split up, Lt Carlos followed one which dropped several bombs near two enemy ships on the south-west side of Kiska – no hits. Lt Dixon joined Lt Rynerson and his wingman, who had been protecting a photo aeroplane, and strafed Little Kiska. They report no sign of life there, but a camp area full of tents etc. The squadron then tacked onto the bombers and returned to base.'

The 11th FS P-40s returned to Umnak later that same day.

Chennault and Boomer (CO of No 111 Sqn RCAF) were each credited with a confirmed victory for the 25 September mission, but it was to be the last aerial combat of 1942 for the Aleutians P-40 pilots. Also during September, the 11th and 18th FSs were assigned to the newly formed 343rd FG and Jack Chennault was promoted to group CO. Joining them in the 343rd FG was a new P-40 outfit, the 344th FS, plus the 54th FS. The 18th FS moved its headquarters from Cold Bay to Adak in December, but the 344th FS, still in the process of organising, would not deploy to the Aleutian chain until early 1943.

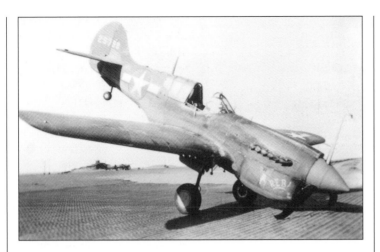

P-40K-5 42-9799 *REBA* of the 344th FS is seen nosed up at Shemya on Marsten mat. The squadron transferred from Umnak to Shemya in June 1943, and also maintained a detachment on Attu as well. Despite inclement conditions in the Aleutians, the operational careers of Eleventh Air Force Warhawks lasted much longer than in other theatres. For example, the RCAF had operated this aircraft from Adak prior to it reverting to USAAF ownership (*Glenn Miller*)

An 18th FS crewman clowns in the cockpit of Maj Clayton J Larson's P-40K at Adak in 1943. The Japanese flag below the windscreen represents the 'Rufe' floatplane that Larson shot down near Amchitka on 18 February 1943. The aircraft is camouflaged in dark green and dark brown over neutral grey, but its serial number is unknown (*Morris Boynton*)

Operations from Adak continued throughout the winter of 1942-43 whenever the weather allowed. P-40s of the 18th FS flew bombing and strafing missions against Kiska while the longer-ranged P-38s ventured all the way to Attu, nearly 500 miles away at the end of the chain. American troops landed on the island of Amchitka in mid-January 1943 and immediately began building a new airfield there. This island, just 75 miles from Kiska and 330 miles from Attu, became the new home of the 18th FS on 15 February, and the 11th FS moved to Adak a few days later.

Japanese float floatplanes from Kiska had been harassing the Americans on Amchitka since they first arrived, making several bombing and strafing raids which caused minor damage and a number of deaths. The arrival of the 18th FS soon put an end to this problem. Squadron CO Maj Clayton J Larson was leading a two-aircraft patrol of P-40Ks on 18 February when he spotted two A6M 'Rufe' floatplane fighters over Saint Majarius Bay off the south-east shore of the island. Larson and his wingman, 1Lt Elmer J Stone, immediately attacked and shot down both 'Rufes'. One fell into the bay three miles offshore and the other one went down off Bird Cape at the south-west end of Amchitka. These were the last confirmed kills by P-40 pilots in the Aleutians during World War 2.

With the aerial threat to Amchitka eliminated, offensive operations against Kiska began in earnest during the spring of 1943. American air-

Maj Art Rice, 11th FS CO between August 1943 and June 1944, scored two victories over Kiska while flying a P-39 with the 57th FS/54th FG in September 1942 (*Joe Connor*)

craft pounded the island incessantly in what became known as the 'Kiska
Blitz'. The 11th FS sent a detachment to Amchitka on 12 March to join
the effort, and it flew 25 missions before returning to Adak on 17 May.

Meanwhile, plans were being formulated to retake Kiska and Attu
from the Japanese. The decision was made to leap-frog Kiska and take
Attu first. American troops went ashore there on 11 May and a bloody
18-day battle ensued before the island could be declared secure. The
island of Shemya, just 40 miles from Attu, was taken at the same time, and
the 344th FS moved a detachment of P-40s to a flat windswept rock pile
on the island on 23 May 1943. Now all the Eleventh Air Force's attention
was focused on Kiska.

By this time, no Japanese aircraft remained to defend the island, so
American aircraft could approach at will, although anti-aircraft defences
were still operable. The 'Kiska Blitz' was kept up through the summer of
1943 as preparations for the invasion of the island took shape. The
Japanese Navy, however, sent a convoy of ships to the island under the
cover of a dense fog and evacuated the garrison on the night of 28 July.
When American and Canadian troops landed at Kiska on 15 August, they
found the island deserted.

**These 344th FS P-40Ks deployed
from Cold Bay to Adak in January
1943 for operations against Kiska.
They display the white spinner and
leading edge unit markings of the
squadron, plus a badge on the
cowling consisting of two
overlapping letter 'Vs' with a
machine gun on white bird's wings
overlaid on top. The P-40K-5 in the
background is 42-9767**
(*Henry Yellott via Butch Yellott*)

**Flat, barren and desolate, Shemya
Island at the western end of the
Aleutian chain was occupied in
August 1943 to provide an airfield
for B-29 strikes against Japan. The
base was never used for that
purpose, but B-24s based there
bombed Paramushira and the Kurile
Islands during 1944-45. Warhawks of
the 344th FS provided air defence**
(*A F Laurie*)

The news of Kiska's evacuation came as no surprise to Capt George I Ruddell, CO of the 18th FS's 'D' Flight. His story starts a few days before the invasion;

'The Jap anti-aircraft fire was usually pretty intense during air attacks. For this reason, when light or no flak activity began being reported by bomber and fighter crews, it seemed likely that the enemy might have escaped from the island. Nevertheless, bombing and strafing attacks continued to be ordered. Finally, after yet another "quiet" mission with four aircraft of "D" Flight, I decided to determine if the flak had really stopped. With the rest of my flight keeping their eyes open for flak activity, I flew with flaps down, "low and slow", over the Jap encampment and gun positions, but saw no activity of any kind. I made a similar check of the Jap runway. There were three not-too-large bomb craters from some previous mission, but it looked okay for landing on the 2000-ft strip (our own runway was only 2600 ft long).

'I checked with the flight to be sure they shared my confidence in our ability to land there safely. Satisfied, we made a wide landing pattern, spaced for each aeroplane to land after the one ahead had stopped and cleared to the side of the runway. My wingman, Lt (Richard) Lee, and the element leader, Lt (John) Bradley, landed safely behind me. No 4, Lt (Warren) Little, Bradley's wingman, landed a bit hot, however, and still had his tail up in the air until just a short distance from the 200-ft drop-off at the end of the runway. He slowed and slid to a safe stop. His heart was not the only one that nearly stopped!

'We got out of our aircraft and walked about the facilities and gun positions, taking pictures and enjoying our little tour. We also a saw a small shrine where, in English, it stated (as near as I can recall), "Here lies a brave American fighter pilot who died for his country". We were greatly surprised at that. We finally took off with no difficulty and arrived back at Amchitka an hour or so overdue.

'Maj Bill Booth, our squadron commander, met my aeroplane with, "Where the Hell have you been?" That was followed with a pretty severe chewing out, plus the news that Col William Elder, our group commander, wanted to see me "right now!" Maj Booth's "irritation" with me

The 11th FS moved from Umnak to Adak in February 1943 to take part in the 'Kiska Blitz'. By the time this photograph was taken later that year, the squadron had stopped applying the elaborate 'Aleutian Tiger' nose art to its replacement aircraft. In the foreground is P-40E-1 41-36150, with three new P-40N-20s next in line. A B-24 taxis out in the background (*Joe Connor*)

Capt George I Ruddell, 18th FS flight commander, led many missions to Kiska, and even landed there prior to the invasion. He then flew a second tour over Europe in P-47s, scoring 2.5 confirmed victories. A decade later he would become an ace in Korea, destroying eight MiG-15s while flying F-86s in the 51st FIW (*Morris Boynton*)

S/Sgt Mike Charles painted the name *Shorty* on this 18th FS P-40K, which was assigned to Lt Clifford D Jolley, and also decorated several other P-40s in the squadron. Jolley flew the aircraft during an uneventful tour at Attu, but he made a name for himself during the Korean War when he shot down seven MiG-15s in 1952 (*Mike Charles*)

Maj Dean Davenport, last wartime CO of the 18th FS, was a veteran of the Doolittle raid on Tokyo in 1942. An extremely popular and effective leader, Davenport flew on the Tokyo raid as co-pilot on B-25 40-2261 *The Ruptured Duck* for 1Lt Ted Lawson, who wrote the classic account *Thirty Seconds Over Tokyo* (*Mike Charles*)

wasn't even a warm-up to what came next. The colonel wrote the book on how to get the attention of a mere captain. Suffice to say, I haven't flown over, or set foot on Kiska, since! Sadly, word of the Japs having left the island did not reach the ground troops, who made a night assault landing on Kiska about a week later. Twenty-two young US and Canadian troops were killed in that attack, mistaking friendly soldiers for the non-existent enemy. Perhaps the lessons to be learned from the realistic attack were considered too valuable to permit knowledge of the enemy's departure to be released. Whatever, each of those men died bravely for his country. The lessons learned were applied to later invasions in the South Pacific.'

George Ruddell finished his tour in the Aleutians shortly after the Kiska invasion, but returned to combat in 1944 flying P-47s with the Ninth Air Force . He scored 2.5 victories over Europe, but greater accomplishments lay ahead for him. Flying F-86s as CO of the 39th FIS/51st FIW in Korea during 1952-53, Ruddell achieved eight more victories. Another future F-86 ace, Lt Clifford D Jolley, also flew P-40s with the 18th FS in the Aleutians.

THE OTHER ENEMY

With the capture of Kiska, the air war in the Aleutians was essentially over. But the three P-40 squadrons would remain in the islands until the end of

White stripes adorn the wingtips and rudder of this 11th FS P-40N-5 42-105104 at Adak. Note also the red border on the national insignias, suggesting that this photograph was taken during the summer or autumn. Only the yellow propeller spinner remains from the earlier squadron markings (*Joe Connor*)

2Lt Robert E Schellhous poses with the 11th FS 'We'll Be There' sign at Adak on a rare sunny day in January 1945. Schellhous, who flew in the 11th and 344th FSs, recalled, 'The only enemy craft I saw were Japanese incendiary balloons. On two occasions I was in the flight scrambled to intercept the balloons, but they were at too high an altitude to fire on in a P-40' (*Bob Schellhous*)

the war, providing air defence to guard against another Japanese attack. The final opportunity for combat came on 11 October 1943, when the Japanese sent a formation of eight 'Betty' bombers from Pamushiru to attack Attu. The 344th FS scrambled its P-40s, but the warning came too late and the 'Bettys' escaped after bombing ineffectually. The P-40's last chance for glory in the Aleutians had passed.

Although the shooting war in the Northern Pacific was over, the weather remained just as formidable a foe as ever. George L Hicks, CO of the 18th FS in 1944, recalled a day when he flew from Amchitka to Shemya and landed just as a dense fog began settling over the airfield;

'Getting out, I told the ops officer to hold all scrambles from the 18th. He informed me that four had just taken off. The last two circled and landed, but the flight leader and wingman had climbed on out. The flight leader, Capt Pete Diefenbeck, was one of our original volunteers. We got in radio contact and brought him over Shemya, which was relatively flat. There was no GCA at that time.

'Pete and his wingman flew over the runway at 200 ft – I heard them pass over but he could not see lights – then climbed back on top at about 4000 ft. This was repeated twice more and Pete lost his cool. He told the wingman, "Make up your f---ing mind!" I got on the radio and told Pete his best bet was to vector back over Attu and bale out. We then got word

Capt Pete Diefenbeck, 18th FS flight commander, wears the DFC he won for leading his wingman through low overcast to a safe landing at Shemya in 1944. The censor has obliterated the artwork on the cowling of the P-40K parked behind him (*Jim Elsner*)

Capt George L Hicks took over this P-40K-1 (42-45831) from Maj William Booth when he assumed command of the 18th FS from Booth in January 1944 at Amchitka. The lower cowling, with its cartoon showing Disney's 'Pluto' urinating on the rising sun, appears to have been transferred from another Warhawk. In the background is *Reina*, the P-40K flown by Capt Fred Beall and crewed by Sgt Morris Boynton (*Morris Boynton*)

These 11th FS P-40Ns stopped at Umnak en route to Elmendorf Field, where they were to be exchanged for P-38s, in the spring of 1945. Note the yellow spirals on the propeller spinners of the first and third Warhawks. One of these aircraft got caught in a quick-moving fog and crashed into Mount Tulik shortly after taking off from Umnak, killing its pilot, Lt Clark (*Carlton Molesworth Jr*)

that a bit more visibility was showing at Alexai Point, so they were sent there with a straight-in approach at 200 ft. Both landed safely, but the wingman ground looped – who cared? I put Pete in for the DFC and his wingman in for the Air Medal. Both were approved. To me, that was flying.'

As the war dragged along through 1944 and into 1945, the P-40 pilots in the Aleutians had little to do but fly occasional practice missions and dream of going home. One of those pilots, Capt William L Morris of the 344th FS at Shemya, wrote a poem, which echoed the nickname of his squadron – 'The Ravens' – and a famous work by Edgar Allen Poe, to capture the essence of his tedious assignment. Titled *Brother – Never More*, the poem is reproduced here with the permission of his family;

This mixed group of 344th FS P-40Es and P-40Ks awaits the scramble order at Shemya in 1944-45. The nearest aircraft is P-40K 42-9830 and the next in line is ex-11th FS P-40E-1 41-36150, on which the vertical fuselage band has been painted out. An AT-6 is parked on the far side of the apron (*Glenn Miller*)

1Lt William L Morris, with 344th FS P-40K *MISS.GERALDINE,* was the poetic pilot who penned *Brother, Never More.* Determined to see combat after leaving the Aleutians, Morris flew P-47Ns in the Pacific with the 463rd FS, and scored one probable victory on 8 August 1945 over Japan (*Richard Morris*)

When it's double zero muck-muck
And the wind's begun to roar
And the ravens are all grounded
'Cause they've spun in before;
So you call up the controller
And bitch and piss and moan
'A whale just buzzed the runway',
You tell him on the phone.
But it's CAVU in Anchorage; Nome is open, too,
The geese took off at Wrangel, so scramble 32.
Fifty dollars for a wingtip but they say that this is war,
Okay, we'll take off this time,
But Brother, Never More.

Falling snow created a speckled effect in this photograph of an 18th FS P-40K at Attu in 1944. The significance of the white checks on the radiator intake lip is unknown, but the yellow front half of the propeller spinner was often seen on 18th FS P-40s (*Morris Boynton*)

APPENDICES

Victories by Units Operating the P-40 in the Pacific Theatre

8th FG
Headquarters – 2 kills
35th FS – August 1943-February 1944 - 50 kills

15th FG
45th FS – January 1942-March 1944 - 11 kills
46th FS – December 1941-early 1942 - 0 kills
47th FS – December 1941-late 1943 - 7 kills
72nd FS – January 1942-late 1943 - 0 kills

18th FG
6th FS – December 1941-January 1943 - 0 kills
19th FS – December 1941-early 1942 - 0 kills
44th FS – December 1941-November 1943 - 117.5 kills
73rd FS – December 1941-January 1943 - 0 kills
78th FS – December 1941-late 1943 - 0 kills

24th PG*
Headquarters - 1 kill
3rd PS* – December 1941 - 2 kills
17th PS – December 1941-April 1942 - 16 kills
20th PS – December 1941-January 1942 -12 kills
21st PS – December 1941 - 3 kills
34th PS – January-March 1942 - 2 kills

Notes
* - re-designated from pursuit to fighter unit in May 1942
** - the 70th FS also operated P-39s during this period

49th FG
Headquarters - 9 kills
7th FS – February 1942-September 1944 - 113 kills
8th FS – February 1942- September 1944 - 152 kills
9th FS – February-December 1942 - 40 kills
33rd PS (Provisional) – February 1942 - 1 kill

71st Tactical Reconnaissance Group
110th TRS – November 1944-February 1945 - 14 kills

343rd FG
11th FS – January 1942-circa June 1945 - 6 kills
18th FS – December 1941-circa June 1945 - 2 kills
344th FS – October 1942-circa June 1945 - 0 kills

347th FG
68th FS – January-April 1943 - 17 kills
70th FS – June-November 1943** - 145 kills

17th PS (Provisional) – February-March 1942 - 43 kills

20th PS (Provisional) – February 1942 - 5 kills

<u>Total USAAF P-40 victories in Pacific Theatre – 655</u>

Aces who flew P-40s in the Pacific

Name	Unit	P-40 Kills	Notes
Capt Robert M DeHaven	7th FS/49th FG	10	(also 4 kills in P-38)
Capt Ernest A Harris	8th FS/49th FG	10	
1Lt Andrew J Reynolds	20th and 17th PS(P), 9th FS/49th FG	9.333	
Capt George E Kiser	17th PS(P), 8th FS/49th FG	9	
1Lt Joseph J Lesicka	44th FS/18th FG	9	
Capt Robert H White	8th FS/49th FG	9	
Capt Frank L Gaunt	44th FS/18th FG	8	
Maj Arland Stanton	7th FS/49th FG	8	
Capt Cotesworth B Head Jr	44th FS/18th FG	8	(also 6 kills in P-38, KIA)
Capt William J Hennon	17th PS(P), 7th FS/49th FG	7	
1Lt James B Morehead	17th PS(P), 8th FS/49th FG	7	
Capt Lucien B Shuler	44th FS/18th FG	7	
Maj William L Turner	20th and 17th PS(P)	7	(also 1 kill in P-400, inc 5 kills CBI)
Major Robert B Westbrook	44th FS/18th FG	7	(also 13 kills in P-38, KIA)
Capt Elmer M Wheadon	44th FS/18th FG	7	
1Lt Richard L West	35th FS/8th FG	6	(also 8 kills in P-38)
Capt Ellis W Wright Jr	49th FG HQ	6	
1Lt James P Hagerstrom	8th FS/49th FG	6	(also 8.5 kills in Korea)
1Lt Robert L Howard	8th FS/49th FG	6	
1Lt John D Landers	9th FS/49th FG	6	(also 8.5 kills in P-51 in ETO)
1Lt Donald W Meuten	8th FS/49th FG	6	(MIA)
1Lt Magnus W Francis	44th FS/18th FG	5.5	
1Lt Lee R Everhart	35th FS/8th FG	5	(also 1 kill in P-38)
1Lt Jack A Bade	44th FS/18th FG	5	
Capt Robert C Byrnes	44th FS/18th FG	5	
1Lt William C Day Jr	8th FS/49th FG	5	
1Lt I B Jack Donalson	21st PS/24th PG, 9th FS/49th FG	5	
1Lt Cyrus R Gladen	44th FS/18th FG	5	
1Lt A T House Jr	7th FS/49th FG	5	
1Lt Henry E Matson	44th FS/18th FG	5	
Capt Grant M Mahony	3rd PS/24th PG, 17th PS(P)	5	(inc 1 kill CBI, also 1 kill in P-51, KIA)
1Lt Boyd D Wagner	17th PS/24th PG	5	(first P-40 ace, also 3 kills in P-39)
1Lt William A Gardner	35th FS/8th FG	4	(also 4 kills in P-38)
Capt Franklin A Nichols	7th FS/49th FG	4	(also 1 kill in P-38)
2Lt George S Welch	47th PS/15th PG	4	(also 12 kills in P-38 and P-39)
1Lt Lynn E Witt Jr	35th FS/8th FG	4	(also 2 kills in P-38)
1Lt Robert W Aschenbrener	8th FS/49th FG	3	(also 7 kills in P-38)
1Lt Elliott E Dent Jr	7th FS/49th FG	3	(also 3 kills in P-38)
1Lt Marion C Felts	8th FS/49th FG	3	(also 2 kills in P-38)
1Lt Joseph J Kruzel	17th PS(P)	3	(also 3.5 kills in ETO)
1Lt Joel B Paris III	7th FS/49th FG	3	(also 6 kills in P-38)
Flt Off Sammy A Pierce	8th FS/49th FG	3	(also 4 kills in P-38)
1Lt Robert H Vaught	9th FS/49th FG	3	(also 2 kills in P-38)
2Lt David W Allen	7th FS/49th FG	2	(also 3 kills in P-38)
2Lt Frank E Adkins	17th PS(P)	2	(also 1 kill in P-39, 2 in ETO)

Name	Unit	P-40 Kills	Notes
1Lt Frederick E Dick	7th FS/49th FG	2	(also 3 kills in P-38)
1Lt Nelson D Flack Jr	8th FS/49th FG	2	(also 3 kills in P-38)
2Lt Kenneth R Pool	35th FS/8th FG	2	(also 3 kills in P-38)
Maj Sidney S Woods	9th FS/49th FG	2	(also 5 kills in ETO)
2Lt Stephen W Andrew	7th FS/49th FG	1	(also 8 kills in ETO)
2Lt Harry W Brown	47th PS/15th PG	1	(also 5 kills in P-38)
1Lt Robert H Moore	45th FS/15th FG	1	(also 11 kills in P-51)
Capt Clifford H Troxell	8th FG HQ	1	(also 4 kills in P-38 and P-39)
1Lt James A Watkins	9th FS/49th FG	1	(also 11 kills in P-38)
2Lt Arthur E Wenige	9th FS/49th FG	1	(also 5 kills in P-38)
2Lt John B Murphy	11th FS/343rd FG	0.5	(also 6.25 kills in ETO)
2Lt George T Chandler	8th FS/49th FG	0	(5 kills in P-38)
1Lt William C Drier	8th FS/49th FG	0	(6 kills in P-38)
2Lt Thomas L Hayes Jr	17th PS(P)	0	(8.5 kills in ETO)
2Lt Clifford D Jolley	18th FS/343rd FG	0	(7 kills in Korea)
1Lt Lowell C Lutton	9th FS/49th FG	0	(5 kills in P-38, KIA)
2Lt George E Preddy Jr	9th FS/49th FG	0	(26.833 kills in ETO, KIA)
Capt George I Ruddell	18th FS/343rd FG	0	(2.5 kills in ETO, 8 in Korea)

Note – This list does not include aces who flew P-40s in Hawaii but not in combat

1

P-40B (serial unknown) 'White 160' of 2Lt George S Welch, 47th PS/15th PG, Haliewa, Hawaii, 7 December 1941

George Welch secured his place in history when he scored four victories on the first day of the Pacific War. The P-40 units in Hawaii were in the process of changing their markings system when the Japanese attacked on 7 December 1941, and the exact scheme worn by the 47th PS P-40 that Welch was flying that day may never be known for certain. Current research suggests this is the most likely candidate. Welch joined the 36th FS/8th FG in New Guinea during the latter part of 1942 and became an ace when he scored three victories while flying a P-39 one year to the day after his Pearl Harbor exploits. He went on to score 16 kills during the war, but was killed while testing the North American F-100 Super Sabre in 1954.

2

P-40E (serial unknown) of 1Lt James O Beckwith, CO of the 72nd FS/15th FG, Hawaii, January 1942

Only 'small-mouth' P-40Bs and Cs (plus P-36s) equipped Hawaiian pursuit squadrons at the time of the Pearl Harbor attack. This P-40E was delivered soon after, and it boasts the very short-lived red and white pre-war-style rudder stripes. The thin stripe on the fin is probably the beginning of a command marking. Beckwith, who named all his aircraft *Squirt* in honour of his daughter, rose to command the 15th FG during its very long range escort operations from Iwo Jima in Mustangs during 1945.

3

P-40E (serial unknown) 'Black 17' of Capt Ed Dyess, CO of the 21st PS/24th PG, Bataan Field, the Philippines, March 1942

No photographic evidence for this aircraft exists. *KIBOSH* was flown extensively by Dyess during the Japanese advance in the Philippines during early 1942. The last P-40 remaining on Bataan, it was flown out by Lt I B Jack Donalson to Iloilo during the Japanese breakthrough on 8 April 1942. Donalson made a wheels-up landing, damaging the aircraft slightly, and it was set on fire a few days later to prevent captured by the enemy. This markings scheme is based on a description left by Dyess – the bright blue patches covered bullet holes. A groundcrewman also recalled painting a skull in a pilot's helmet and scarf on both sides of the forward fuselage in about the middle of March 1942. Dyess would be captured by the Japanese on Bataan, but later escaped to fight with Filipino guerrilla troops.

4

P-40E (serial unknown) 'White 14' of 1Lt Joseph J Kruzel, 17th PS (Prov), Blimbing, Java, February 1942

Kruzel scored his first three victories during the Allies' unsuccessful defence of Java in early 1942. His P-40E displays the first application of his dragon nose-art, which he later used on the starboard side of his Warhawk in the 9th FS/49th FG. It may also have had a yellow rudder. Other Java P-40Es included Maj Charles A Sprague's *Hell Diver;* Lt N H 'Cy' Blanton's 'White 17', Lt J R Hague's *Kathleen* and Lt W J Hoskyn's *Stub and Lou.* Sprague, Hague and Hoskyn were killed in Java, while Kruzel and Blanton went on to serve both in the 49th FG and in the European theatre, where Kruzel increased his final score to 6.5 confirmed victories.

5

P-40E (serial unknown) 'White 36' of Capt William J Hennon, 7th FS/49th FG, Darwin, Australia, Summer 1942

Hennon, the only American pilot to score five victories over Java, flew this P-40E after transferring to the 7th FS/49th FG in Darwin. Of interest are the red spinner, which many Philippines and Java veterans in the 49th FG painted on their aircraft, the stars around the nose, the flight leader's band around the rear fuselage and the large 'Bunyip' screaming demon design, which the 7th FS later adopted, on the rudder. This aircraft was eventually wrecked in a collision. Hennon went on to score seven victories before completing his combat tour, and he later disappeared on a cross-country flight in March 1943 after returning to the US.

6

P-40K-1 42-45966 'White 24' of Capt Franklin A Nichols, 7th FS/49th FG, Port Moresby, New Guinea, March 1943

USAAF P-40s did not only wear sharkmouths in China. Nichols, a Pearl Harbor survivor, flew this P-40K while serving in New Guinea as a flight commander, operations officer and deputy CO in the 7th FS/49th FG. It carries the nickname of his *NIP NIPPERS* red flight on the cowling and twin command stripes on the rear fuselage. Nichols transferred to the newly-formed 431st FS/475th FG, flying P-38s, in June 1943, and scored his fifth, and last, victory with that unit. He made a career in the USAF, retiring in 1970 as a major general.

7

P-40K-1 42-46292 'White/Blue 29' of 2Lt Arland Stanton, 7th FS/49th FG, Port Moresby, New Guinea, March 1943

Stanton was a replacement pilot who joined the 7th FS/49th FG in the autumn of 1942 in New Guinea, where he was assigned to Nick Nichols' 'Nip Nippers' flight. He scored his first victory on 30 November 1942 over Buna while flying with Nichols. In his second combat, flown in this aircraft on 6 February 1943, Stanton shot down a Zero and damaged a Kawasaki Ki-48 'Lily' bomber during a big scrap near the forward airstrip at Wau. Exactly one year later, on 6 February 1944, the young Pennsylvanian scored his fifth confirmed kill.

8

P-40N-5 (serial unknown) 'White 20' of Capt Arland Stanton, CO of the 7th FS/49th FG, Gusap, New Guinea, February 1944

Stanton was appointed CO of the 7th FS/49th FG in November 1943, taking *KEYSTONE KATHLENE* as his personal aircraft. It had the name *Empty Saddle,* accompanied by nose art showing a reclining nude woman, on the lower right cowling, and also displayed the white tail and leading-edge markings adopted by the Fifth Air Force in the summer of 1943. He was flying the aircraft on 6 February 1944 when he achieved ace status with a single kill while escorting A-20 strafers over Muschu Island. Stanton scored three more times during the spring of 1944 to bring his final victory tally to eight confirmed and one damaged during his long combat tour.

9

P-40N-5 (possibly 42-105405) 'White 13' of 1Lt Robert M DeHaven, 7th FS/49th FG, Gusap, New Guinea, late January 1944

Bob DeHaven would score ten of his eventual fourteen victories in P-40s of the 7th FS/49th FG, making him equal top of the list of USAAF Warhawk aces in the Pacific theatre. He scored his first victory in a P-40K on 14 July 1943 and his fifth in this aircraft on 10 December. Like many aircraft in the squadron, it carried different nose art on each side of the nose, with a white and purple orchid painting on the lower left cowling and *Rita* in white script on the lower right cowling. The crew chief has installed a fresh-air venturi intake below the cockpit of this machine. DeHaven later flew two other P-40Ns before converting to the P-38, with which he took his score to 14 confirmed victories. He became a test pilot after the war and he also served as president of the American Fighter Aces Association.

10

P-40N-5 (serial unknown) 'White 24' of 1Lt Elliott E Dent Jr, 7th FS/49th FG, Gusap, New Guinea, late January 1944

Dent scored the first of his three P-40 victories on 3 July 1943, just six weeks after joining the 7th FS/49th FG. His next chance to score came six months later, on 23 January 1944, when he shot down two Zeros near Cape Torabu. He achieved three more victories during a single mission in November 1944 after his squadron had transitioned to P-38s. The red border on the national markings of Dent's P-40N identifies it as a replacement aircraft delivered to the 49th FG in late 1943 – the name *Anne The B'ham Special* on the cowling refers to the city of Birmingham, Alabama, where Dent went into business after the war.

11

P-40N-5 (serial unknown) 'White 7' flown by 1Lt Joel B Paris III, 7th FS/49th FG, Hollandia, New Guinea, May 1944

Paris was one of thousands of young Americans who signed up for flight training in the months immediately following the Pearl Harbor attack. Two years later he was a pilot in the 7th FS/49th FG, with whom he scored his first confirmed victory, over a Ki-43 'Oscar', over Wewak on 13 March 1944. Paris achieved a total of three victories in the P-40N, signified by three Japanese naval ensigns stacked vertically below the cockpit of his aeroplane. He continued scoring after the squadron got P-38s, finishing the war with a total of nine confirmed victories.

12

P-40E-1 41-36171 'White 61' of 1Lt James B Morehead, 8th FS/49th FG, Darwin, Australia, 25 April 1942

This very plain P-40E-1 was typical of the aircraft flown by the 49th FG in the opening months of the defence of Darwin.

Morehead, who had scored his first two victories during the fighting in Java, was credited with shooting down three Japanese twin-engined bombers in this aircraft on 25 April 1942 as a member of the 8th FS/49th FG. Morehead was thoroughly shot up by Zeros during the fight and crash-landed near Adelaide River. He was unhurt, but the P-40 never flew again. His next aircraft was 'White 51', nicknamed *'L'Ace'*. After completing his tour in the Pacific, Morehead went back to war flying P-38s in the Mediterranean theatre, where he scored his eighth, and last, victory on 6 June 1944.

13

P-40E (serial unknown) 'Yellow 57' of Capt George E Kiser, 8th FS/49th FG, Darwin, Australia, May 1942

'King' Kiser, considered by many contemporaries to be the best fighter pilot in the south-west Pacific, was already an ace when he joined the 8th FS, having destroyed two enemy aircraft in the Philippines on the third day of the war and three more during the Java campaign. His P-40E in the 8th FS, photographed at Darwin in May 1942, carried his personal lion ('king of the jungle') artwork, seven red dots representing his victory total at the time', and the red forward spinner denoting a Philippines/Java veteran. It also reportedly had its two outboard machine guns removed to save weight and improve manoeuvrability. Kiser scored nine victories in the Pacific. He returned to combat in 1944, flying P-47s in the European theatre, but did not add to his score.

14

P-40E-1 41-35972 'Yellow 43' of 1Lt William C Day Jr, 8th FS/49th FG, Dobodura, New Guinea, March 1943

Bill Day served in the 8th FS throughout the unit's defence of Darwin but did not score his first victory before moving to Port Moresby on 1 November 1942. On 11 March 1943 he shot down a 'Zeke' and a Mitsubishi G4M 'Betty' off the coast of New Guinea for his fourth and fifth victories, making him the first 8th FS pilot to become an ace in New Guinea proper. Day spent some 28 months in the south-west Pacific area before returning to the US in April 1944. This P-40E, the second assigned to Day, carried the name *MARY-WILLIE* on right side of its nose, and had four yellow bomb 'spokes' on each wheel centre.

15

P-40E-1 (serial unknown) 'Yellow 42' of 1Lt Nelson D Flack Jr, 8th FS/49th FG, Dobodura, New Guinea, May 1943

A Pennsylvanian, Flack learned to fly with the Royal Canadian Air Force before transferring to the USAAF in March 1942 to complete his training. He joined the 8th FS/49th FG in May 1943 at Dobodura, where he was assigned this P-40E. Flack did not score in it, but on 7 November 1943 he shot down a 'Zeke' and probably got another while flying a P-40N. His second Warhawk kill came over a Kawasaki Ki-61 'Tony' on 14 February 1944, but he was shot down in the fight and broke his arm when he crash-landed in the jungle. After returning to combat Flack scored three further kills in P-38s.

16

P-40E-1 (serial unknown) 'Yellow 49' of Capt Ellis W Wright Jr, V Fighter Command headquarters, Dobodura, New Guinea, May 1943

Wright earned his wings in 1940 and was stationed in Hawaii at the time of the Pearl Harbor attack. He joined the 49th FG in late 1942 as 8th FS operations executive, often flying this colourful P-40E. He transferred to V Fighter Command as assistant operations director in March 1943, by which time he had three confirmed victories to his credit. On 11 April 1943 Wright shot down three Zeros in a single engagement while defending shipping at Oro Bay, taking his victory total to six. He rotated back to the US in June 1943, but returned to combat during the Korean War.

17

P-40E 41-5648 'White 59' of 2Lt Robert L Howard, 8th FS/49th FG, Dobodura, New Guinea, May 1943

Howard joined the 8th FS at Dobodura in late 1942. On 7 January 1943, flying this P-40E, he downed a Zero and claimed a second as a probable, but he was shot up in the fight and had to make an emergency landing without flaps or brakes. The aircraft was not badly damaged, however, and Howard went on to score four further victories in it by 14 May 1943. JAYNE CARMEN was named after Howard's girlfriend, and it carried the name Gremlin's Rendezvous on the right side of the nose. Howard scored his sixth, and last, victory in a P-40N on 21 September 1943.

18

P-40E-1 41-25174 'White 54' of 2Lt Robert H White, 8th FS/49th FG, Dobodura, New Guinea, May 1943

Bob White left his home in Kansas City, Missouri, to join the USAAF as an aviation cadet just five days after the attack on Pearl Harbor. Like Bob Howard, he joined the 8th FS in late 1942 and scored his first five victories between 7 January and 14 May 1943 to join the growing list of aces. During the 14 May interception at Oro Bay, White scored one of 13 victories credited to the 8th FS, a feat which earned the squadron the first Distinguished Unit Citation to be awarded to an individual squadron during the World War 2.

19

P-40N-5 (serial unknown) 'Yellow 55' of 2Lt Sammy A Pierce, 8th FS/49th FG, Marilinan, New Guinea, August 1943

Pierce's KAY was amongst the first batch of P-40Ns assigned to V Fighter Command in the summer of 1943, these aircraft being sent to New Guinea to replace ageing P-40E/Ks. Pierce had already scored three confirmed victories by this time. He flew this P-40N, which carried the name HAILEAH WOLF on the right side of nose, for several months, but did not claim any confirmed victories in it. After completing his first combat tour in May 1944, Pierce served briefly as a test pilot in the US before returning to the 8th FS. On 26 December 1944, he shot down four Japanese fighters to bring his final total to seven confirmed victories.

20

P-40N-5 42-104947 'Yellow 67' of Maj Ernest A Harris, CO of the 8th FS/49th FG, Marilinan, New Guinea, November 1943

Double ace Ernie Harris was one of the top P-40 pilots of the Pacific air war. He was known for more than just his 'stick-and-rudder' talents, however, as members of the

8th FS considered him to be the best squadron commander in the business. This aircraft replaced Harris's P-40E in the summer of 1943, and he scored his last confirmed victory in it on 21 September 1943, plus an unconfirmed 11th kill two months later. Harris was killed in a jet fighter crash in 1949 while serving in Germany.

21

P-40N-5 42-104990 'Yellow 42' of Capt Robert H White, 8th FS/49th FG, Marilinan, New Guinea, November 1943

A four-month scoring drought came to an end for White not long after he received this P-40N, his third KANSAS CITY KIDDIE, when he shot down two 'Bettys' and a 'Tony' on 6 September 1943 near Lae, New Guinea. He scored once more, taking his total to nine confirmed victories and one probable, before completing his combat tour in December 1943.

22

P-40N-5 (serial unknown) 'Yellow 46' of 1Lt Robert W Aschenbrener, 8th FS/49th FG, Marilinan, New Guinea, December 1943

Aschenbrener was just beginning to make his mark in the 8th FS as veteran aces such as Harris, Howard and White were completing their combat tours. Flying this P-40N, which was named after his mother, Aschenbrener claimed his first two victories on 15 November 1943 when he shot down an 'Oscar' and a 'Zeke' near Gusap. He scored once more in the aircraft before converting to P-38s, and eventually ran his score to ten confirmed and one damaged.

23

P-40N-5 42-105834 'Yellow 51' of 1Lt Donald W Meuten, 8th FS/49th FG, Gusap, New Guinea, April 1944

Meuten was another replacement pilot who joined the 8th FS in late 1943 and soon began running up a score. Flying this rather plain P-40N, he recorded six confirmed victories between 15 November 1943 and 12 March 1944, when he was credited with a triple kill during a fight near Wewak. Meuten disappeared in this aircraft on 7 May 1944 shortly after moving with his unit to the recently captured airfield at Hollandia.

24

P-40E-1 41-24809 'White 83' of 2Lt I B Jack Donalson, 9th FS/49th FG, Darwin, Australia, June 1942

Donalson scored three confirmed victories over Nichols Field, in the Philippines, on the first day of the war, and later escaped to Australia. There, he joined 'Blue Flight' of the 9th FS/49th FG, and participated in the defence of Darwin. This was the first of Donalson's two P-40Es named MAUREE. It had a white spiral design on its wheel centres. He scored one victory in this aircraft on 14 June 1942, then wrecked it in a twilight landing two days later. Donalson scored his fifth kill on 30 July flying the replacement MAUREE, Warhawk 41-36090.

25

P-40E-1 (RAF serial probably ET503) 'White 86' of 1Lt Andrew J Reynolds, 9th FS/49th FG, Darwin, Australia, July 1942

91

Reynolds was the first high-scoring P-40 ace of the Pacific air war, achieving 9.333 confirmed victories between 6 February and 30 July 1942. His first kills came during the Java campaign before he joined the 9th FS in Australia. Soon appointed commander of 'Blue Flight', Reynolds became an ace on 4 April when he shot down a Japanese bomber and a Zero which were raiding Darwin. His distinctively-marked Warhawk – actually a reverse-Lend Lease Kittyhawk – carried the name *Oklahoma Kid* on the right side engine cowling.

26
P-40E serial 41-5647 'White 81' of 2Lt John D Landers, 9th FS/49th FG, Darwin, Australia, Summer 1942
Another member of Andy Reynolds' deadly 'Blue Flight', 'Big John' Landers scored his first six confirmed victories in the 9th FS during 1942. His P-40E, *SKEETER*, in which he scored his first four kills, mimicked the gaudy diving eagle on Reynolds' aircraft. After completing his combat tour in the Pacific, Landers went on to achieve greater fame as commander of several Eighth Air Force fighter units. He finished the war with a total of 14.5 confirmed victories.

27
P-40E-1 41-24872 'White 94' of 1Lt Robert H Vaught, 9th FS/49th FG, Darwin, Australia, Summer 1942
A former enlisted cavalryman, Vaught was a member of the original cadre of 9th FS pilots who sailed for Australia in January 1942. He scored three confirmed victories in P-40s, then finished with two more in 1943 after the squadron converted to P-38s. Vaught's *"BOB'S ROBIN"* was one of four sharkmouthed P-40Es in the 9th FS. The name was repeated on the other side of the fuselage, which showed considerable signs of patching and repainting.

28
P-40E 41-5316 'White 72' of 2Lt James A Watkins, 9th FS/49th FG, Darwin, Australia, June 1942
'Duckbutt' Watkins flew in the 9th FS throughout the defence of Darwin, but did not score his first victory until 26 December 1942, by which time the unit had moved to New Guinea. Photographs of his P-40E suggest it was one of a small number of Warhawks which displayed the white star national insignia without the blue disc within it. It also had a cartoon of 'Donald Duck' pulling a parachute on the lower right cowling, a reference to Watkins' nickname. He eventually ran up a score of 12 confirmed kills, all but the first of which were accomplished with the P-38.

29
P-40E-1 41-25163 'White 74' of 1Lt Sidney S Woods, 9th FS/49th FG, Darwin, Australia, Summer 1942
Woods, another original member of the 9th FS, was injured in a landing accident in late March 1942 and was assigned this aircraft upon his return to duty after a month's medical leave. He scored no victories in the aircraft, which displayed the name *KIP* on the left side of its rudder, but scored twice in P-38s before completing his tour in the summer of 1943. Woods returned to combat with the Eighth Air Force's 4th FG (as its deputy group CO), claiming five further victories during a single combat in March 1945. He was shot down while strafing shortly thereafter and finished the war as a PoW.

30
P-40N-5 42-105506 'Yellow C' of Maj Emmett S Davis, CO of the 35th FS/8th FG, Tsili Tsili, New Guinea, January 1944
Davis earned the nickname 'Cyclone' during 1941 while stationed in Hawaii, where his peers considered him the hottest Army pilot among them. In the summer of 1943, as recently appointed CO of the 35th FS/8th FG, Davis engineered the conversion of his unit from P-39s to new P-40Ns, claiming 42-105506 as his own. He scored his first victory on 27 September 1943 and two more on 26 December 1943. In the latter action, Davis believed he had destroyed at least five Japanese aircraft, but only received confirmation for two. He flew P-38s as commanding officer of the 8th FG, but he had no further opportunities to score.

31
P-40N-5 42-105745 'Yellow Y' of 1Lt Richard L West, 35th FS/8th FG, New Guinea, February 1944
West, whose flying skills and fighting spirit matched those of Davis, was the first pilot in the 35th FS to become an ace. He scored his first two victories on 22 September 1943, with four more on 15 November 1943, when he was credited with two 'Oscar' fighters and two 'Sally' bombers during a wild fight near Kaiapit, New Guinea. The name *LUCKY* was added on both sides of the nose some weeks after the four-victory mission. West went on to score a further eight victories after the 35th FS re-equipped with P-38s in 1944.

32
P-40N-5 42-105502 'Yellow S' of 1Lt Roy A Klandrud, 35th FS/8th FG, New Guinea, February 1944
The 35th FS scored no fewer than 65 confirmed victories during the four months that it operated P-40Ns, and Klandrud was credited with three of them. His Warhawk displays the standard squadron markings of yellow propeller spinner and aircraft letter, plus three Japanese flags below the cockpit, signifying Klandrud's single victories on 22 September, 26 November and 26 December 1943. Klandrud returned to the US in October 1944 after completing 196 combat missions with the 35th FS.

33
P-40F-15 41-19831 'White 209' of 2Lt Lucien B Shuler, 68th FS/347th FG, Guadalcanal, April 1943
Bob Shuler flew 33 combat missions with the 68th FS between February and May 1943, when a bout of malaria forced him out of the cockpit. At the time his aircraft displayed the distinctive sharkmouth markings of the 68th FS, along with the short-lived P-40 theatre markings on the tail, which were replaced by an all-white tail in June 1943. After three weeks of treatment, Shuler joined the 44th FS/18th FG, in which he flew P-40M 'White 107' *Georgia Peach*. He began scoring almost immediately, claiming seven victories in two months, including four 'Zekes' on 4 August 1943 over Munda. The ace was wounded on 31 December 1943 flying a P-38 and was sent home shortly afterwards.

34
P-40M (serial unknown) 'White 126' of Capt Frank L Gaunt, 44th FS/18th FG, Guadalcanal, July 1943

As the 44th FS used up its P-40Fs during the summer of 1943, they were replaced by Allison-powered P-40Ms such as this one assigned to Frank Gaunt, a former pre-med student. Gaunt had no opportunities for aerial combat during his first six months on Guadalcanal, but he scored seven victories in *The "TWERP"!* during the summer of 1943. He completed his score with a victory in a P-38 on 11 January 1944, before returning to the US. Gaunt flew a second combat tour on P-51s in the Mediterranean theatre, but did not add to his score.

35

P-40M (serial unknown) 'White 125' of Capt Joseph J Lesicka, 44th FS/18th FG, Munda, August 1943

Lesicka had already scored three victories in four months with the 44th FS when he took off on a mission over the invasion beach at Munda, on New Georgia Island. His patrol met a large formation of Japanese bombers and fighters, and in a hectic 20-minute engagement he shot down five enemy aircraft. Lesicka was the second 44th FS pilot to become an 'ace in a day', as 1Lt Elmer Wheadon had accomplished the feat on 1 July 1943. Lesicka's aircraft was named after burlesque star Gypsy Rose Lee, this being a reference to the fact that the P-40M was 'stripped' of weight in an attempt to improve performance. It also had a diving eagle design painted on its white wheel centres.

36

P-40F (serial unknown) 'White 111' of 1Lt Jack A Bade, 44th FS/18th FG, Munda, September 1943

Bade joined the 44th FS in Hawaii in 1942 and deployed with it to Guadalcanal in late January 1943. The squadron had its first battle with the Japanese a week later, and Bade scored his first confirmed victory on 4 February. He achieved his fifth, and final, victory on 30 June 1943, but continued to fly with the squadron until September, when he returned to the US. Bade's 'White 111', which was one of the last P-40Fs in the squadron, carried the name *Reckless Prostitute* and 14 Japanese kills flags on the right side of its fuselage.

37

P-40K-1 42-45746 'White 33' of 1Lt Robert W 'Todd' Moore, 78th FS/15th FG, Kauai, Hawaii, Summer 1943

Moore arrived in Hawaii in September 1942 fresh from flight training and flew P-40s in the islands for more than a year before moving to the Gilbert and Marshall islands. This well-worn P-40K – the first of Moore's seven *Stingers* – carries the markings of the 78th FS/15th FG. Moore scored his first victory on 26 January 1944 while flying P-40Ns with the 45th FS. In 1945, flying Mustangs on very long range operations from Iwo Jima, he claimed 11 more confirmed victories to become the top scoring pilot in the Seventh Air Force.

38

P-40N-5 42-105109 of 1Lt Dwight R 'Bob' Butler, 45th FS/15th FG, Apemama, Gilbert Islands, February 1944

The P-40Ns operated in the Gilbert Islands by the 45th FS/ 15th FG were notable for their unusual camouflage scheme, which was apparently chosen to blend with the sand on the barren islands. Butler and the other 45th pilots flew mostly ground attack missions during the campaign, but on 26 January 1944 they had a fierce encounter with Japanese fighters while escorting B-25s attacking Taroa airfield, on Maleolap Atoll. Butler claimed one confirmed victory in the fight, his only one of the war. *"TWEEDIE II"* was the second fighter which Butler named after his wife.

39

P-40E 40-601 of 2Lt John J Cape Jr, 11th FS/28th CG, Umnak, Aleutian Islands, 4 June 1942

The P-40s of the 11th FS were devoid of unit or personal markings when the squadron flew its most famous engagement, the defence of Dutch Harbor on 3/4 June 1942. Cape shot down a Zero over Umnak Pass on 4 June while flying 40-601, but he was then shot down and killed. Subsequently, the airfield on Umnak Island was named in his honour. Note the shroud on the exhaust pipes, which was part of the cold-weather equipment installed on the aircraft. In the summer of 1942, the 11th FS decorated its P-40s with a gaudy Bengal tiger's head on both sides of the engine cowling.

40

P-40K 42-45831 of Capt George L Hicks III, CO of the 18th FS/343rd FG, Amchitka, Aleutian Islands, January 1944

Hicks joined the 18th FS after more than a year of instructor duty in Florida. Flying from Amchitka Island, he participated in the last fighter strike against Kiska before its capture on 15 August 1943. Hicks had a personal insignia painted on the nose of his P-40K which depicted the Disney character 'Pluto' urinating on the rising sun. Incredibly, someone at Eleventh Air Force headquarters objected to the design and ordered the rising sun painted out! Typical of P-40s in the Aleutians, 42-45831 had a long operational life. Delivered to Alaska in March 1943, it remained on operations until 15 March 1945, when it was condemned for salvage.

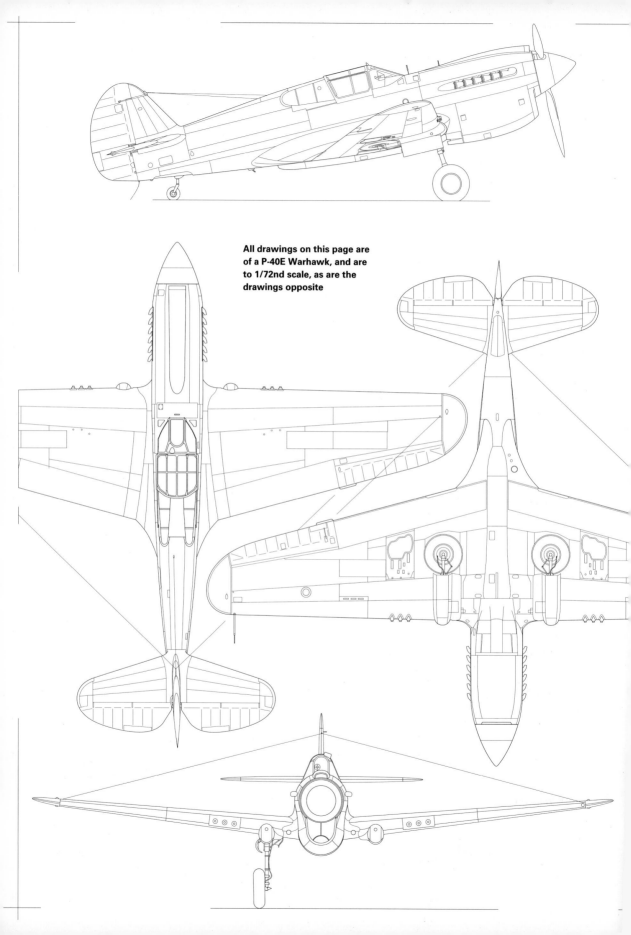

All drawings on this page are
of a P-40E Warhawk, and are
to 1/72nd scale, as are the
drawings opposite

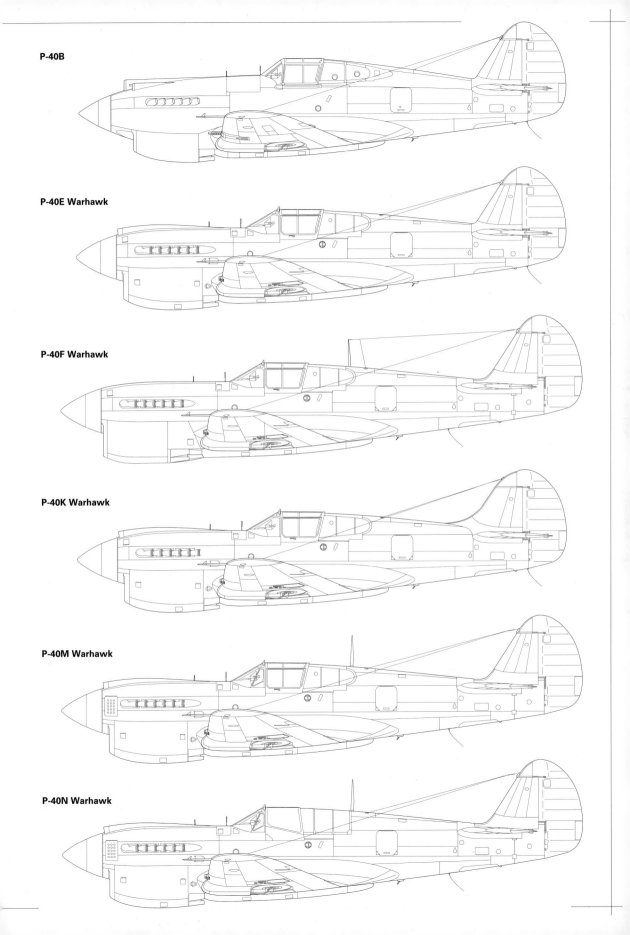

P-40B

P-40E Warhawk

P-40F Warhawk

P-40K Warhawk

P-40M Warhawk

P-40N Warhawk

INDEX

References to illustrations are shown in **bold**. Plates are shown with page and caption locators in brackets.